God's Pursuit of You

**"A Clarion Call, Beckoning The Church
To Return To Its Center"**

God's Pursuit of You

"A Clarion Call, Beckoning The Church To Return To Its Center"

LEWIS FISHER, JR.

SpeakLife
Publishing

God's Pursuit of You

ISBN: 978-0-615-58656-4
©2012 by Lewis Fisher, Jr.
All rights reserved.
Printed in the United States of America.

Published by SpeakLife Publishing

SpeakLife
Publishing

"The Words I Speak, They Are Spirit and Life."
John 6:63

www.SpeakLifePublishing.com
1-888-596-3882

Post Office Box 1791   Elizabeth City, NC 27906

Acknowledgements

I acknowledge the Holy Spirit, my true teacher and guide. I also acknowledge all those the Lord has used to speak into my life over the years, for I am a culmination of all of you.

Dedication

I dedicate this book to my wife Tonja. She has truly been an inspiration and a stabilizing force in my life, family, and ministry. She inspired me greatly over the years by her walk before the Lord in her private life. To witness such commitment to the Lord sharpened my life, and encouraged me to keep on the path God had chosen for me. God used her to encourage me to keep pursuing kingdom living, kingdom ministry and the completion of this work.

GOD'S PURSUIT OF YOU

Table of Contents

Preface

Over the years, I have participated in and witnessed a church that often appears to thrive on itself, its abilities, and accomplishments; even at times, carrying on as though it is self-existent, and therefore, self-governing. Even to this day, it seems that this posture is being perpetuated through much of the church. We must never forget that we exist because of God alone. We were not, and are not, the center of God's plan. He is! Why is this important? Because we as a people can become conceited and arrogant, thus, demonstrating a self-centered mentality, a position of thinking that everything is always about us.

Well my dear friend, the plan of redemption has always been about God; we are simply beneficiaries of His grace. As God is self-existent, He decided He would favor humanity. Why? He did so because He could. He decided to pursue us and shower us with all that He is. How dare we now act as if He is subservient in the relationship? Webster's Dictionary defines subservient as "being in a position of secondary importance." Think about that. If one is of secondary importance, what they want, need, etc, is not at the top of another's list. In my view, that has been the problem with the church; God has been in a position of secondary importance. It appears, at times, that what He wants and needs is not the primary concern of His people, a people He has given so much to save. I liken our relationship this way; we consider God as a spare tire, only using Him when needed. There is no intimacy from this prospective. How would you feel if people only communicated with you when they needed to use you or your resources? You would probably avoid them after a while because you realize you are not important to them. How much more does the Father withdraw Himself from us, not allowing us to find Him because He realizes that He is not important to us?

The Lord spoke through Jeremiah the prophet saying:

"And you will seek me and find me, when you search for me with all your heart." Jeremiah 29:13

Consider this same verse from The Message Bible translation.

"When you come looking for me, you'll find me. Yes, when you get serious about finding me and want it more than anything else." Jeremiah 29:13

Wow! Isn't that powerful? We will find Him when we want it more than anything. That's the key my brothers and sisters, when we want it more than anything. We MUST return to our true center! God the Father is our center, and what He wants and needs must take center stage. Only when this is a reality in our lives will we see the manifestation of all that He is. We must be determined to convince the Father of our need for Him as much as we need air to breathe. Let us no longer live by a "Check Box" mentality. We routinely just go through the motions, attending the various services or events just to feel good about ourselves, and are not really concerned about having a real relationship with the Father through Jesus Christ. By this approach, the spirit of our enemy has lulled many to sleep by a false sense of being pious (devoutly religious). This mindset has, and can render one blind to what the true church of Jesus Christ is, and what it should be doing. In many ways this view can render the church to being nothing more than an organization, rather than a living organism full of life. As the church, the body of Christ, we must understand that our existence is only in Him, and that His life is to flow through the body for which He died. Let me emphasize again, that a church that is self-centered will not be the influence in the earth that it is capable of.

A few years ago, I found myself frustrated and no longer content with the routine of Bible Study, Sunday Bible School, and morning worship. I began sensing that there was something more for me. Have you ever felt like that? Does it fit where you are now? Church as usual was not bringing any satisfaction, so I knew a change was needed. Deep within me there was a hunger for much more than what I was experiencing on a personal and corporate level. I didn't realize initially why I had such frustration, but then the Lord revealed to me that He had created a purer hunger in me. This newfound hunger was not for more church services, functions, or activities; it was for God the Father. I realized that I was transitioning from a life centered on Lewis, to one that longed only for my Father. I was no longer content with much serving; I needed to hear His voice.

Remember, at one point in her life, Martha tried serving the Lord through much activity. What she found out, just as I did, and perhaps you, too, that much activity breeds much frustration when it is initiated and maintained from a man-centered prospective. Listen to me my friend. Everything we do MUST begin and be sustained by God if we expect His influence. You see, Martha was doing a noble thing; she was waiting on the Lord. However, she never asked Him if that was what He wanted.

> *"And Jesus answered and said unto her, Martha, Martha, thou art careful and troubled about many things. But one thing is needful: and Mary hath chosen that good part, which shall not be taken away from her." Luke 10:41-42*

Are you busy with much activity? Does frustration grip you to the very core of your being as you serve? I was no longer content with doing things for show, having a form of godliness, yet never producing anything of any eternal value. I saw nothing in my life that was worth talking about. I had been an utter failure as a believer. Armed with this awareness of my failure in life, I made a conscious choice to truly answer the call of the Lord and commit to Him in my private life. Once I did that, everything changed. I realized for the first time that I was not the center of my life, the Lord Jesus Christ was. Now I understand that we say this routinely, however, for me, it became a reality for the very first time, and I had knowledge of it. I began experiencing true victories over those things that held me captive for so many years. I have learned that what I am to God in public is what I am in private. True victory begins with a life of Holiness. God has prescribed a successful plan for our lives, and it begins, continues, and ends with Him, not you and me. For years now I have been committed to preaching a Christ Centered message that emphasizes life in private, rather than in the open forum.

Thus, I have written this book, in the hope that it will encourage you the reader, to see the need to change your approach to God, and where you have Him in your life. That is, in order of precedence, is He first, second, third, etc? I pray that you recognize that He is Holy and that He is the only one capable of bringing forth a people that can reproduce Him in the earth. But He will not respond to being second in our lives. Are you really ready to answer the call of a Christ Centered life? If so, then read on! Let the Lord of Glory be revealed to you as you take this journey with me. I assure you, you will not be the same.

Lewis Fisher, Jr

xiv

INTRODUCTION

"You have not chosen me, but I have chosen you." John 15:16

In any relationship, there must be a signal sent to the potential mate that alerts them to the fact that one is interested in him or her. According to the words of our Lord Jesus Christ, The Father, through Him, sent the signal to humanity. Simply put, He (The Father) took the first step in the hope of establishing a life-long relationship with man. This is extremely important, as it keeps us grounded and focused more on His abilities and actions more so than our own, or the lack thereof. This aforementioned principle of relationship highlights our dependency on Him to bring the relationship to what He envisioned it to be.

"Being confident of this very thing, that he which hath begun a good work in you will perform it until the day of Jesus Christ." Philippians 1:6

That being said, too many messages we hear over the radio, television, internet, and in many books, seem to allude to the audacious fact that perhaps humanity took the first step in the relationship with Christ we now enjoy. Jesus is vividly clear that the Father took the first step, a point I will emphasize throughout this writing. As a launching place, I want to share with you how God made His advances toward me, and my responses to His gracious advances.

I was born to Lewis and Dora Fisher of Merrimon, North Carolina, during the year of 1961. Merrimon is a small community located in Carteret County. To say it is rural is an understatement. I grew up with four brothers and three sisters. We had a happy childhood by all accounts. I admired my dad so much because he worked very hard to take care of his family. In my view, his work ethics were second to none. My mom also worked long hours away from home to help make ends meet. They were emphatic about making us go to church on Sunday morning. We attended a small community church called Reels A.M.E. Zion. We also attended other denominations from time to time.

I remember questioning why I had to attend church services, when all I saw afterwards suggested that none of what went on inside the building carried over outside the building. I witnessed men and women with a great commitment to attending services, activities and events; however, the commitment was not equally ingrained in the lifestyles outside the walls of the building. After all, an old adage was passed through generation after generation, that is, just do the best you can; God will understand. That was the attitude then, and it seems to be the attitude now. It suggests that we do the best we can do, with regards to holy living. It did not matter if we were living in a habitual sin state or not, as long as we made sure we attended the service in the building on Sunday. If we did this, everything would be all right. Beloved, the best you and I can do outside of our heavenly Father is to commit sin.

Please understand this, God will not understand!!! The reason He will not understand is because of the steps He has taken to deliver us. He knew the best we could do, and that effort had us on a collision course with hell. Jesus came on the scene, issuing orders for us to alter our course. He then provided the means to do so, by the offering of Himself, and with His blood, He marked and sealed the permanent course of life for us. His sacrifice enabled us to effectively alter the course of our lives.

If you will, we were a vessel underway, operating outside the prescribed navigational channel. You see, many waterways in the United States and abroad are marked with the appropriate buoys, markers, etc. These aids to navigation are in place to make sure those navigating on 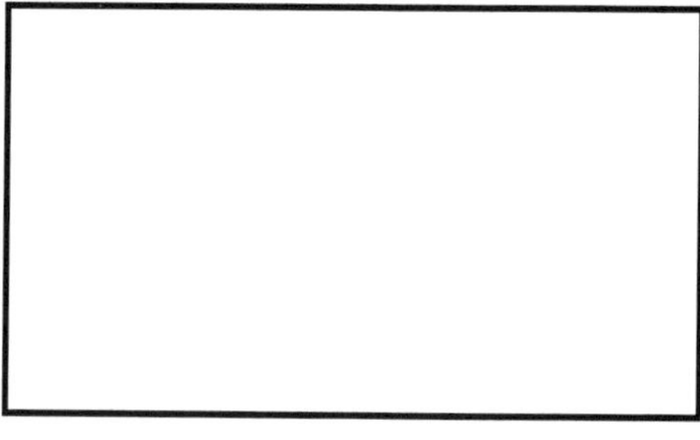 the water do so within the channel as marked, for their safety and for the safety of others. Operating inside the channel minimizes the risks of inflicting harm upon self and others. Outside the channel, one runs the risk of running aground or worse.

Without Jesus, we operate outside the safety of the channel, and our lives are run hard aground as a result. Even worse, we put the lives of those within and without our circle at risk. Every thing we do outside the will of God puts others at risk! Thank God that Jesus came and issued those new orders to put us back on course and in the realm of safety. We needed a saviour that could live this holy life through us.

We Were Without Hope In This World!

"Wherefore remember, that ye being in time past Gentiles in the flesh, who are called uncircumcision by that which is called the circumcision in the flesh made by hands; That at that time ye were without Christ, being aliens from the commonwealth of Israel, and strangers from the covenants of promise, having no hope, and without God in the world." Ephesians 2:11-12

What a powerful picture of grace. We had no true identity without Jesus Christ and we were in no position to receive of His bountiful blessings. Yet, He looked upon us with love, and as a result of that look, He sacrificed Himself, that we who were not a people could be ingrafted into the family of God. He adopted the Gentiles as sons and daughters; they no longer needed to live without identity in the world.

He Delivered Us From Death And From Living

I must make this point at this juncture; He not only delivered us from death, He delivered us from living. The apostle Paul summed it up like this:

> *"I have been crucified with Christ, nevertheless I live, yet not I, but Christ liveth in me, and the life which I now live in the flesh, I live by faith of the Son of God, who loved me and gave himself for me." Galatians 2:20*

No matter how much dad and mom made me attend services, there was no change in my heart and character, mainly because I did not have a true encounter with Jesus Christ. Yet, He pursued me. Even while my lifestyle suggested that I did not need or want Him, He pursued me. What a loving God! How many of us would have been that persistent to woo a potential mate, especially after being rejected time after time? The truth is, we probably would not have been.

Recognition of Pursuit

It is extremely important in any relationship to recognize when you are being pursued. If one is not aware of pursuit, think about the potential loss and the life that could have been, but was not because of the lack of one's ability to perceive they were being pursued. As I reflect on how God pursued me, it is truly humbling.

I remember when I first recognized God's pursuit of me. It took place while I was serving as a boat crewman at Fort Macon, the United States Coast Guard Base located in Atlantic Beach, North Carolina, in 1981. The boat crew had just returned from a Search and Rescue mission. I was tired, so I decided to turn in for the evening. I seemed to have fallen asleep pretty quickly. I remember hearing a sound in the corner of my room, nothing loud, but enough to let me know I was not alone in the room. I remember raising my head to see who or what was making the noise. As I looked in the corner of the room, I saw a bright light; it was in the silhouette of a man. I remember attempting to speak, but could not. The image of this man just stood there for a minute or so. Then, as quickly as the image appeared, it vanished. Needless to say, I was initially struck with fear, but then overwhelming curiosity. I thought for a moment that perhaps I had lost my mind. Little did I know that my kinsman redeemer was pursuing me? I did not speak of the encounter with anyone; I mean, who would believe me?

Shortly after that, perhaps a week or so if my memory serves me well, I had my second encounter by way of a dream. I dreamed that in the midst of the clearest sky I had ever seen, and the purest white clouds, there was a giant Bible. The pages of the Bible were turning, and I asked, "What is this?" Then suddenly the pages stopped turning and highlighted the following word of the Lord:

> *"And Jesus came and spake unto them, saying, All power is given unto me in heaven and earth. Go ye therefore, and teach all nations, baptizing them in the name of the Father, and of the Son, and the Holy Ghost. Teaching them to observe all things whatsoever I have commanded you: and lo, I will be with you always, even unto the end of the world. Amen." Matthew 28:18-20*

I was again overwhelmed, and wondered if this meant that a person with my history of sin was being told to go and preach.

There was no desire in me to be in church, let alone preach. I am so grateful, beloved, that He took the first step.

Although I saw no need for Him, He was not at all dissuaded in His pursuit of me. He had a purpose for me, and it was clear He wanted me to know what it was. Like Jonah of old, God intended that he go to the wicked city Nineveh and cry unto it. Well, the scriptures record that Jonah had no desire to follow the orders given him. Little did he know that God would not change His mind about him, and that no matter what God had to do to get him there, He was going to do it. Well, after many attempts to circumvent God's plan for him, Jonah eventually surrendered. He went to Nineveh!

Well, I could not shake what had transpired to this point, so I built up enough courage to tell my dad and mom about this. I remember clearly what my dad said, "Boy don't be saying you are something that you are not." I knew my dad meant well; he did not believe in playing with the Lord. Since I, too, had doubts as to what these things meant, I figured it would be best if I just kept quiet about it.

Not long after my talk with my dad, I dreamed again. During this third and final encounter, God the Father showed me a white church building. In the dream, I approached the building, and as I drew near to the entrance, the doors opened, and there I was standing behind the pulpit. Then my Lord spoke to me saying, "Go, for now you know that I have sent you." I recall having a very numb feeling. I was reluctant to tell my dad, so I went to tell my grandmother, the late Lillie Mae Morris. As I began telling her about the three encounters I had, she started thanking and praising the Lord. She told me that God told her that He was calling one in her family to preach the gospel. Grandmother encouraged me to follow the call of the Lord.

I set out to find the church building the Lord revealed to me, and I found it. The name of the church was and is to this day, Great Joy Worship Center, located in Beaufort, North Carolina, where Ezekiel Murrell, Jr. serves as Senior Pastor. As I entered the building, I felt a move of the spirit I was not accustomed to.

The move of the Holy Spirit upon me had such a profound impact that I gave my heart to Jesus and accepted His pursuit of me. I joined that local church body and served faithfully under the leadership of the set man of God. The Lord used him to lay the proper spiritual foundation in my heart, making me better fit to serve. I am so glad I yielded to His advances; my life has never been the same. Likewise, you, too, are being pursued by a Holy God. Give in to His advances and live.

ENDNOTES/SCRIPTURES

1. John 15:16
2. Philippians 1:6
3. Ephesians 2:11-12
4. Galatians 2:20
5. Matthew 28:18-20
6. Kelley Varner, Principles of Present Truth from Genesis, Praise Tabernacle Printing, 1992

1

GOD'S PURSUIT OF YOU

"While we were yet without strength, in due time Christ died for the ungodly."
Romans 5:6

I mentioned early on in this writing, in relationships, there must be a first move.

He Made the First Move

One's intentions must be made clear to the potential recipient. Say this with me, "God so loved the world that He gave." Did you notice what I did not say? I did not say the world so loved God that it gave. The greater (God) condescended to the lesser. He left eternity to come and live in a world based on time. Why? He wanted to live among His people, to be up close to them. His arrival and actions would be the evidence of His love for us. I say again, God first loved us! I know we quote this all the time, so it is not strange to our ears, but I wonder how many of us have caught a revelation of it. You see my dear friends, revelation cannot be taught; it must be caught by the spirit. Does it really resonate within our hearts? We were not looking for Him, nor did we want Him. I am grateful that His love compelled Him to act nonetheless.

> *"Christ arrives right on time to make this happen. He didn't, and doesn't, wait for us to get ready. He presented himself for this sacrificial death when we were far too weak and rebellious to do anything to get ourselves ready."*
> *Romans 5:6 (The Message Bible)*

Praise the name of the Lord! Aren't you glad the Lord did not wait for us? Think about this for moment. Our Lord acted in faith, creating an avenue back to Himself, believing that we would one day come to our senses and acknowledge His finished work. He had to act, because we were in no position to help ourselves. God the Father made the first move in preparing the opportunity for fellowship.

Can you imagine where we would be if God had waited for us to get ready? As The Message Bible says, we were rebellious and too weak to get ourselves ready. Why is it then that we, by our selfish actions, attempt to dominate the relationship, as if we came to Him, and that we have given the most? How do we dominate the relationship? We dominate it by thinking that everything is always about us. As mentioned in the Preface, we put our God and what He needs in the secondary position. I tell you why we do it. Because the same spirit that moved upon Lucifer is moving upon the hearts of men and women around the globe. He is trying to get us to think more highly of ourselves than we ought to. He thought he should usurp God and receive the glory that belonged only to God. That was an eternal mistake!

> *"How art thou fallen from heaven, O Lucifer, son of the morning! How art thou cut down to the ground, which didst weaken the nations! For thou hast said in thine heart, I will ascend into heaven, I will exalt my throne above the stars of God: I will sit also upon the mount of the congregation, in the sides of the north." Isaiah 14:12-13*

Are we not doing the same thing? How so you might ask? When we think that what we will takes precedence over what He wills. Have we not exalted ourselves above Him? Have we not moved upon the same principle as Lucifer? We must return to our center! As a people, His will MUST take precedence! Are you willing to move Him from the subservient position? I know some would argue this point of view, but I submit to you, If God is not first, who or what is?

He Showed Up with a Today Message

God showed up in the flesh, not as man was expecting Him to. You see, man was expecting Him to arrive with glory and splendor, but our God took a less desirable path. He came in obscurity, in the small town of Bethlehem, born of a carpenter and his betrothed. This was certainly not the lineage one would think about first.

The enemy, as you well know, tried time and time again to snuff out the life of Jesus Christ before He could fulfill His purpose. Thank God he was unsuccessful in stopping our Father from legally entering into the earth realm.

> *"In the beginning was the Word, and the Word was with God, and the Word was God. And the Word was made flesh, and dwelt among us, and we beheld his glory, the glory as of the only begotten of the Father, full of grace and truth." John 1:1, 14*

> *"Then said I, Lo, I come, (in the volume of the book it is written of me), to do thy will, Oh God." Hebrews 10:7*

God took on flesh. He revealed Himself to us in the person of Jesus Christ to announce His remedy for sin and to show us how to have a relationship with Him. The trumpet of truth is sounding! Can you hear it? The trumpet with clarity communicates and highlights not man's initiatives and actions, but rather the initiatives and actions of God our Father. The Father longed for fellowship, so He sent His son Jesus to prepare the way. He (Jesus) showed up to the worship service with this powerful announcement:

> *"The spirit of the Lord is upon me, because he hath anointed me to preach the gospel to the poor; he hath sent me to heal the brokenhearted, to preach deliverance to the captives, and recovering of sight to the blind, to set at liberty them that are bruised. To preach the acceptable year of the Lord."*
> *Luke 4:18-19*

I want to emphasize the fact that everyone in the synagogue loved the message Jesus was reading from the book of Isaiah. Using the vernacular of today, they would be saying, preach Jesus preach! That is until Jesus brought light to His message as it related to time. He said in verse 21, *"This day is the scripture fulfilled in your ears."*

As long as they thought the message was futuristic, they were with it. However, when Jesus said *today*, it placed a responsibility on the hearers to act upon it. They, like the people of our day, are most comfortable talking about something with a futuristic outcome. It is easy to delay any required action when results are not expected NOW, TODAY! The spiritual landscape has changed! No longer are we without strength or hope. We lose now because we choose to, not because it has to be that way. A man-centered point of view will disagree with me, but those whose hearts are open to Him know that there is something sound in what I am saying. You and I cannot afford to lose anymore. In every circumstance, whether it be persecution, distress, tribulation, or peril, we are NOW made to win and overcome them, especially after all God has done to change the spiritual landscape. The apostle Paul wrote:

> *"Nay, in all these things we are more than conquerors through him that loved us."*
> *Romans 8:37*

I Say Unto Thee Rise Up

People are crying out for deliverance from spiritual tyranny, and unfortunately, their governments are not in a position to meet the demand of their cry; that's where the church comes in. No longer are we going to ignore what we see happening in the earth, but rather, we will rise and take our place of dominion, and bring relief to those that need it. This is possible because of the first step God has already taken to establish Himself in a people. Consider an excerpt from Prophet Bernard Jordan's book "Written Judgments:"

> *"It is a day when the Church world will no longer bury its head in the sand, but will open its eyes and address issues and confront situations in a measure never before seen."*

I believe this day is upon us. However, revelation of this can only come by way of the spirit. When we regain balance, that is, when we are centered in Christ, we will see that His victory is our victory, and we can stand in Him! Jesus said plainly:

> *"Dwell in me, and I will dwell in you. [Live in me, and I will live in you.] Just as no branch can bear fruit of itself without abiding in (being vitally united to) the vine, neither can you bear fruit unless you abide in me." John 15:4 (Amplified Version)*

I want to emphasize the meaning of the word, "abide." According to the Merriam-Webster Dictionary, abide means to bear, endure, dwell, remain, and last. I think it's fair to say that many of us have not remained or lasted with Christ; being totally dependent upon Him and His finished work. Therefore, the benefits that were made available to us are not realized. This is why, as a people, we have been struggling, and in many cases losing ground, and have not had any real answers to the world's dilemma or our own. How can we bring deliverance to a people when we ourselves are in captivity to our own will and way? Jesus was crystal clear about putting the cart before the horse, so to speak. He told us to get the beam out of our own eyes, then, we can see clearly to help others. I call this walking in authority. You see, when you are not bound by anything, you can speak with boldness on whatever the subject is. If you are held captive to a particular thing, then, rest assured, you will not speak with any real authority. That being said, whatever has been lost can be recovered.

Time to Recover All

All is not lost though. We, like David, can recover all if we return to our true center, the Lord Jesus Christ. Consider David's plight. The Amalakites ravaged the south and Ziglag, they took the women and children, and burned the place with fire. In I Samuel 30:8, David inquired of the Lord and received consolation from Him:

> *"And David inquired at the LORD, saying, Shall I pursue after this troop? Shall I overtake them? And He answered him, Pursue: for thou shalt surely overtake them, and without fail recover all. □"*

When the Lord is not in a subservient role, He will cause us to take back everything we have lost. Return son, return daughter, to the true center of your joy and strength. It is time to recover all! The Lord declared to David, without fail, you shall recover all! It may sound like a broken record each time I challenge you to return to our true center, but it is necessary. Remember my beloved; faith comes by hearing, not by having heard something once. This is the premise behind my repeating the phrase, "Return to our true center." When we can recognize, and keep focus on a Christo-Centric (Christ Centered) purpose, then it will garner the attention of the Lord and bring His power and resources to bear.

Many individuals and ministries have existed for years without any demonstration of His power or resources. We like quoting the familiar scripture found in Psalm 50:10, "God has cattle upon a thousand hills." Well, if He has them, and we are His children, why don't we have one of them?

If asked why the church does not prosper, a common theme emerges, and that is, it will take more time, or the people are doing the best they can. Often, it is extremely difficult to face the truth of our inability. However, we need to turn to this truth, for it will make us free. Man-centered ministries will not produce the power necessary to free creation. We are to operate as our older brother did, totally dependent, not on His own ability, but on that of the Father's.

As He Is, So Are We

Man-centered ministries are steep in the traditions and philosophies of men. The word "tradition" means custom, ritual, belief, practice, or innovation. It is centered on man's ability, and that, my beloved, counters God's plan for His church. He wants His church dependent upon Him alone. Man-centered ministries paralyze the people, leaving them crippled, and without hope. It disqualifies them from receiving an unlimited provision from God. We must sound the alarm in this hour, in the hope that many will adjust their priorities and shift back to the only ministry God will respond to and endorse, a Christ Centered one. Until we can do this from our hearts, we are going to be in a cycle where we win sometimes and lose sometimes. This was never in God's will for His people. We have been made for dominion from the time of our Genesis face, or the beginning of time.

> *"And God said, Let us make man in our image, after our likeness: and let them have dominion over the fish of the sea, and over the fowl of the air, and over the cattle, and over all the earth, and over every creeping thing creepeth upon the earth."* Genesis 1:22

This announcement of dominion speaks to our heritage in Christ; however, the manifestation of this heritage is based upon principle. The principle of which I speak is mainly, we shall have no other God before Him. The church would be well served to acknowledge the truth of Revelation 1:8; that is, that God is Alpha and Omega, the Beginning and the End. If we believe the scriptures, then we believe God is all the scriptures declare Him to be. If we believe all it says about Him, then we must conclude that what He also said about us is true, that is:

"...As He is, so are we in this world." I John 4:17

We are the visible representation of our heavenly Father. Praise His Name!

> "And God said, *"Let there be light: and there was light. And God saw the light, that it was good: and God divided the light from the darkness. And God called the light Day, and the darkness he called Night. And the evening and the morning were the first day." Genesis 1:3-5*

Now we see by evidence of the scriptures that light was presently in existence on the first day. How can this thing be? There is no mentioning of the sun or moon to this point. Where did the light come from? I'll tell you where it came from. The light came from the almighty God, who is light! On the fourth day, Genesis 1:14-19 declares the bringing forth of the two great lights, one to rule the day, and the other to rule the night; what we know to be the sun and the moon.

How powerful is this! To know that you and I are in the likeness of the one who brings forth life and light from Himself. Child of God, this same power is at work in the believer. If you and I are losing at anything, we need to ask ourselves, why? We were made to dominate, conquer, subdue! Say this with me, **"I am made like God, the Father, therefore, I am made to dominate, conquer, and to subdue all things! I am not made to lose at anything! In Jesus Christ, I have been made victorious!"**

ALL GOD, ALL MAN

Jesus was not limited to the confines of this world, even so we, when the situation calls for it, can rise above the confines, or laws that govern this world. Remember Jesus when He commanded the disciples to go to the other side in

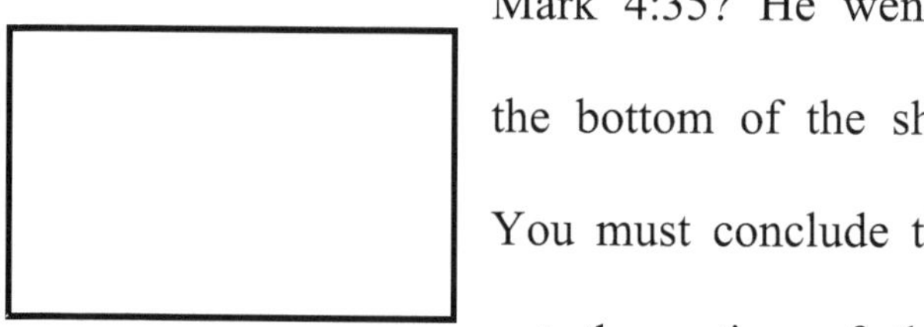

Mark 4:35? He went down into the bottom of the ship to sleep. You must conclude that this was not the action of the only true God, but a man. Beloved, the Bible is clear that God neither slumbers nor sleeps. However, when the disciples feared for their lives, they came to Him saying, "Master, carest thou not that we perish." The same man rose up from SLEEP, stood on the bow of the ship and said, "Peace be still." Guess what. That was not mere man that did that. That was God! He is all God and all man. We are after His kind! He rebuked them because in His words to go to the other side was the ability to get there. Likewise, whatever God has commanded you to do has in it the ability and resources to do it. The disciples did not recognize the power that resided in them. You, too, my dear brother and sister are so clothed with the Father. How long will you

accommodate losing? You are of His seed! You have His word which carries His ability! Now is the time to use it!

Abraham's Seed

In Luke 13:10-16, we find the very seed of God living beneath what her royal heritage provided. That is, by nature of her identity alone, she was afforded the right to be loosed. As we explore the scripture's details of the event, we find a woman who has carried an infirmity for far too long. Consider the following:

> *"And, behold, there was a woman which had a spirit of infirmity eighteen years, and was bowed together, and could in no wise lift up herself."*
> *Luke 13:11*

How long have you suffered so needlessly? As she could not help herself, neither can you do it alone. She not only suffered physically. Think about the emotional bombardment waged against her. Even though she was in the midst of people, she probably felt like an outcast. Have you ever been there? Surrounded by people, yet inwardly, because of your infirmity, you feel like an outcast? Does not this very scene depict a person with no hope? Does it paint your picture? Good news my friend! A new day has dawned. There is a solution, and His name is Jesus! She no doubt heard of Jesus, and because she was in the right place at the right time, He saw her. The Bible tells us that He called to her. She answered His call by coming to Him, and when she did, she heard these powerful words, "Woman, 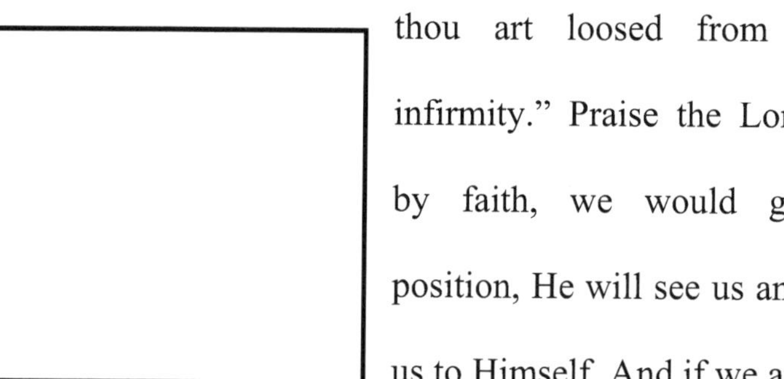 thou art loosed from thine infirmity." Praise the Lord! If, by faith, we would get in position, He will see us and call us to Himself. And if we answer His call and approach Him, we, too, will hear the same words, "Thou art loosed from thine infirmity." Jesus brought deliverance to her 18-year imprisonment by satan. How long have you been imprisoned?

The leaders and the people complained about what Jesus did. After hearing their complaints, He said:

> *"And ought not this woman, being a daughter of Abraham, whom Satan hath bound, lo, these eighteen years, be loosed from this bond on the Sabbath day?" Luke 13:16*

Jesus let them know plainly, her heritage entitled her to a much better life. What about you? Will you be loosed from your imprisonment? Do you belong to Christ? If so, then the word has something to say about you:

> *"If ye be Christ's, then are ye Abraham's seed, and heirs according to the promise." Galatians 3:29*

My friend, you have been eating and drinking from the wrong stall. Jesus has come with revelation of who we truly are. He led us away from the stall of satan, back to the stall of the one true God. Choose to walk into your true heritage in Christ. Be loosed, in the name of Jesus Christ!

"HELLO SEED OF ABRAHAM!"

ENDNOTES/SCRIPTURES

1. Romans 5:6
2. Isaiah 14:12-13
3. John 1:1,14
4. Hebrews 10:7
5. Luke 4:18-21
6. Romans 8:37
7. John 15:4
8. I Samuel 30:8
9. Genesis 1:22
10. Revelation 1:8
11. I John 4:17
12. Luke 13:10-16
13. Galatians 3:29
14. Bernard Jordan, Written Judgements, (Tulsa, OK: Zoe Ministries, 1989)
15. Amplified Bible, Zondervan Publishing (Grand Rapids, MI, 1987)

2

BEGINNING OF PURSUIT

"There was a lamb slain before the
foundation of the world."
Revelation 13:8

As I mentioned early on, we all understand the fundamental principles of relationships between a man and a woman. If a relationship is going to begin, then someone has to initiate it. More simply put, someone has to make the first move. Very seldom do we see both making a move simultaneously. One must be willing to step out to initiate and secure what they hope to be a lasting relationship. That initiative is taken without any assurance that the advance will be received. It might be a look, something said, or the slightest gesture to the party of interest. If the action of the initiator is received, there will be corresponding action from the recipient. Contrary to popular opinion, we did not initiate the relationship we now enjoy. It was all on God! When did this relationship between God and creation begin?

Before Time, He Died

Understand, my friend, it is indeed a difficult concept to grasp in the flesh. Revelation 13:8 reveals that the Lamb was slain before the earth was founded, before it took physical shape. Think about that--how God demonstrated His love for us and His desire to have a lasting relationship with us. He made the first move to establish an eternal relationship with (us) creation. He did it in eternity, then, He manifested what He did in eternity in this time space world. Let me put it another way, when Jesus died on the cross at Calvary, that was a manifestation of what God did before time! Now, ask yourself this question, why would Jesus need to die before we came into existence in this world? Because God, being Omniscient, knows all. He saw man's departure from Him before He ever did it. He took again a preemptive position, to ensure we had a way back to Him. Is this not a powerful picture of our God? Our Father initiated a plan to redeem us before we knew we needed redemption.

What an exhibition of real love! We marvel at the novels written of love by the authors of our time, yet, there is not a love story that can compare to the one the Lord has made known to us in the Holy Scriptures. His love was demonstrated without our consent. Jeremiah the prophet records God's knowledge of us before we were ever in the embryonic stage of existence:

> *"Before I formed you in the belly, I knew thee, and ordained you a prophet to the nations."*

Jeremiah 1:5

"Before I shaped you in the womb, I knew all about you. Before you saw the light of day, I had holy plans for you: A prophet to the nations-that's what I had in mind for you."
Jeremiah 1:5 The Message Bible

The Father, who knows all, saw our actions before one was ever taken. I thank God that He did not have to wait for our consent to act. In His love, He secured our lives and planned out what we were to be and how we were to contribute in this world.

Unilateral and Bilateral Agreements

Let's take a look for moment at what these two agreements have to do with the actions of our loving Father and our actions or the lack thereof. As we consider God's actions on our behalf in eternity past and in time, they speak volumes to each of these agreements. One agreement requires the consent, or actions of another, while the other holds one party responsible for establishing and carrying out the particulars of the agreement. Since God took measures, or if you will, the first step, to establish a relationship, His actions alone ensured man that he did not have to be lost. His actions were unilateral. By definition, a unilateral agreement is a contract in which only one party makes an express promise, or undertakes a performance without first securing a reciprocal agreement from the other party. As I mentioned above, He acted without our consent, without any promise from creation (us); that is, He had no promise that we would accept what He had done for us. Yet, had God not taken measures in eternity, man would not have had an avenue back to Him. In a unilateral agreement God did what man was unable to do; He made redemption possible by the slaying of the Lamb (Jesus).

There was no bilateral agreement, that is, God did not ask man to agree with Him, nor aid Him in making redemption possible. By definition, a bilateral agreement is a contract between parties in which both parties are bound by the exchange of promises. You see my friend, He did not say, man, if you do this, I will do this or that to redeem you. The Omnipotent God decided that all on His own. Praise God! He is the self-existent God that decided man was worth saving even before man thought he needed saving. How dare we carry ourselves in such an arrogant way, to think that we will use God only when we need Him? It's almost as if we have a sign that reads, "Break glass only in time of need, or if war breaks out."

Ray Comfort and Kirk Cameron, the authors of *The School of Biblical Evangelism*, use the example of persons driving above the speed limit; however, they have no knowledge that they actually broke the speed law. They are, to their surprise, visited by a police officer highlighting their transgression of the speed law. The police officer offers consolation to the transgressors by telling them that someone they didn't know paid the speeding ticket for them. Having knowledge of this unilateral action, most of us would attempt to find the person that paid the price of our transgression. It wouldn't matter whether we knew the person or not. How much more should we get to know the One who paid the price for us, without us ever knowing Him, or even before we had knowledge of our transgression? That's why I want to emphasize in this book the actions of our loving Father--actions that took place when we were without hope. Let us be open to this new sound in the spirit and to understand we owe all to our kinsmen redeemer, not religious, man-centric ideals.

When it pertains to any form of religious practice, man believes he has a handle on things. Over the past 26 years of ministry I have come to know just how little we know and how much there is to learn about God. That's not to say that in our day that we do not know more than our ancestors, but it is clear that we see less of God's power in demonstration in our day. Scholars of our time have written books and commentaries that have provided great accounts of God and how man has pursued God. It is not my intention to discredit those that have gone before me. On 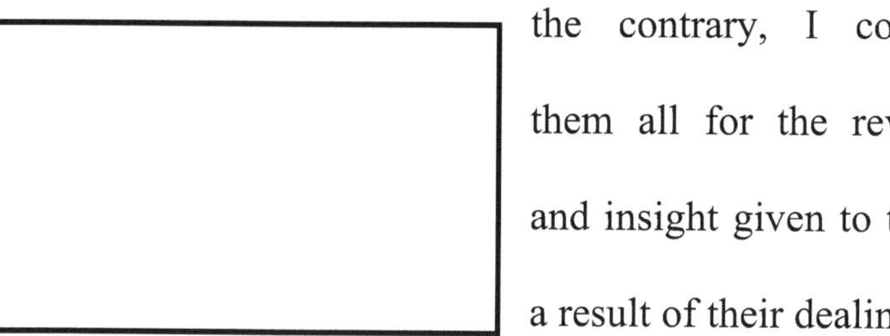 the contrary, I commend them all for the revelation and insight given to them as a result of their dealings with God. However, in this book I want to emphasize the mere fact that God has pursued us before time, His pursuit continues in our time, and this is the reason we have hope. The scriptures, I believe, are replete with evidence that supports my assertion, and that is, that it has been God trying to woo us to be His people.

The decision that we are the people of God is a conclusion in the mind of God, but it seems at times that it is not settled in our hearts and minds. In Deuteronomy 16:16, God declares that He would visit with man three times, or that He has spoken to us excellent, threefold things. There will be three levels of His abiding and each of these levels represents three levels of maturity in our relationship with Him. He also spoke through the apostle Paul that He would finish the relationship, or bring to completion what He has begun.

> *"Being confident of this very thing, that he which hath begun a good work in you, will perform it (complete it) until the day of Jesus Christ."*
> *Philippians 1:6*

Be comforted my beloved. Don't be discouraged in where you are now. Be confident that He will finish what He HAS BEGUN! Do your part in obedience to His word and He will do the rest. Again, He alone took the initiative that sparked the firestorm for an eternal relationship and He will ensure it is completed to the desired standard He alone has set. I am convinced that the principle of the first move is a key to understanding the Lord, our place in Him and in the world. God has been, and always will be, the initiator and sustainer of our relationship.

Grace in the Bread Crumbs

The fairy tale of Hansel and Gretel provides a picture image that I hope will linger with you. It is of Germanic origin and it details the plight of two children living with those that did not love them. They were taken in the woods in the attempt to get them lost so they would never make it back home. However, in his ingenuity, Hansel kept little white pebbles that he dropped along the way so that during the night they would be able to find their way home. I call it the trail of breadcrumbs.

We have been separated from God the Father; so much so, we have no chance of making it back to Him on our own. So, the Lord left a trail of breadcrumbs along our paths to guide us. These breadcrumbs are actually advances the Father has been making on us in the hope that we would recognize His attempt to establish a relationship.

As I look back over my life, I realize that our Father's advances, whether I accepted or rejected, have always been there for me. Think about that my dear friend! God the Father has made advances on us all, and many of us will not find our way back home because we are either ignoring, not recognizing, or outright rejecting the breadcrumbs He has set in our paths. And when we do this, we are rejecting Him. In either case, the person who rejects Him will invariably spend eternity in torment without hope of escape. And that means they will live forever tormented by the evil one. Look around you my dear brothers and sisters; can you see the breadcrumbs? Like Elisha prayed for his servant Gehazi, I pray that the Lord open your eyes that you might see the trail of breadcrumbs He has left just for you, so that one day you can make it back home to Him. He is actively waiting, so that you can experience the joy of establishing a lifelong relationship with the Almighty God.

Once we have established a relationship with the Father, we must understand our place in the relationship. That is, He is the lead and center of it. This will be repeated throughout this book because this principle of being Christo-Centric is vital to our living victoriously in this world. He wooed us in eternity past. What do you mean by that Brother Fisher? He moved to slay the Lamb on our behalf before the world was. What a powerful picture of God's sovereignty and omniscience!

As I mentioned, He preempted the plan of redemption. We can see God as He moves to cover the sin of Adam and the entire scope of humanity in the garden. You see, when Adam sinned and brought about a breach in the relationship, it was God who initiated steps to reconcile (bring back) the relationship. He had to slay an innocent victim to cover Adam and Eve's nakedness. This action pointed to the sacrifice of Jesus Christ, that, as their nakedness was covered, He would cover our nakedness caused by sin.

I remind you, the visible action of the Lord our God in the garden and at Calvary was simply a manifestation of what He had already done in the invisible realm. Think about it. What step could Adam have taken to reverse his actions, actions that plunged humanity into sin? God had no other recourse. At the very moment Adam had eaten from the forbidden tree of the knowledge of good and evil, humanity was plunged into sin and death, and he was helpless to change it. Thank God the Lamb was already slain before the foundation of the world and His coming declared as a result of Adam's fall.

> *"And the Lord God said unto the serpent, because thou hast done this, thou art cursed above all cattle, and above every beast of the field; upon thy belly shalt thou go, and dust shalt thou eat all the days of thy life. And I will put enmity between thee and the woman, and between thy seed, and her seed; it shall bruise thy head, and thou shalt bruise his heel."*
> *Genesis 3:14-15*

In the above scripture, it literally means He (Jesus) shall bruise, or crush, the head of the enemy. The announcement of the defeat of satan is a victory cry for creation. The fact of the matter is, God did what we were helpless to do over 2000 years ago, so why do we now think we can carry out His plan without Him? How is it that we think we have a ministry without Him? Is this not the ultimate position of conceit? We have even structured our local churches, not based upon the word, but on man's idea of how things should be operated. Consider this for a moment. We have established By-Laws, policies and programs that at the very core are contrary to the word God has already established for His church. Is there any wonder why so many believers and local churches live defeated lives?

Listen to me! We were never meant to lose! The moment Jesus shed His blood for us, our victorious life was sealed. If the death of Jesus alone had sealed our redemption, then Jesus would have allowed Himself to be stoned. The fact of the matter is that He was destined to die the death of the cross. Jesus knew that He could not allow death to come upon Him until He reached the cross. You see, we all came under a curse as a result of Adam's sin. If Jesus died from being stoned or during a beating, you and I would still be under a curse. Our enemy, satan, had no idea the cross would unleash such a harvest in the earth. Had he known, he would have ensured Jesus died during the beating. I am so grateful that Jesus' will to please the Father was strong enough to out-duel the evil one. He successfully made it to the cross and when He did, He became a curse for us. Hallelujah! He became a curse for us!

> *"Christ hath redeemed us from the curse of the law, being made a curse for us: for it is written, cursed is every one that hangeth on a tree." Galatians 3:13*

You see, my dear friend, He could not have died any other way! When the soldiers flogged Him, thank God He willed to live. Once on the cross, He willingly gave up the ghost. When He did, darkness covered the earth because the light of the world had gone out. The sun refused to shine. For three days, Jesus remained in the heart of the earth. He suffered in our stead. After His resurrection, when He had made an offering as the perfect sacrifice, redemption was still not complete. Jesus had to do something else. He had to now assume the role as High Priest.

Remember, the Old Testament is filled with types and shadows that point to Jesus and His finished work. That is, the tabernacle pattern on earth was a type of the real one in heaven. As there was a mercy seat on earth, there is one in heaven. Are you beginning to get the picture? In Moses' tabernacle pattern, each year the high priest would enter the Holy of Holies, which is often referred to as the Most Holy

Place, and sprinkle the blood of the sacrifice upon the mercy seat.

Jesus, our newly crowned High Priest, went back to the cross and the other places He had lost blood. He then took the blood of the sacrifice, mainly His own blood, into the Most Holy of All. Then He began to sprinkle the mercy seat, thereby obtaining and sealing our eternal redemption. Praise His holy name! This same Jesus has become both Lord and Christ. He was first the sacrifice, and when He fulfilled that role, He assumed the role as the High Priest, and once He fulfilled all that God required, He was crowned Lord of all! Will you respond to what He has already done on your behalf, or will you continue to try making it on your own? Choose the life He has purchased for you. Synchronize your walk with His will!

ENDNOTES/SCRIPTURES

1. Revelation 13:8
2. Jeremiah 1:5
3. Deuteronomy 16:16
4. Philippians 1:6
5. Genesis 3:14-15
6. Galatians 3:13
7. Ray Comfort and Kirk Cameron, the authors of "The School of Biblical Evangelism", 1993
8. Merriam-Webster's Collegiate Dictionary-10th edition, 1993

3

THE TABERNACLE REVEALS HIM

"And let them make me a sanctuary; that I may dwell among them." Exodus 25:8

There is so much to be said about the Tabernacle of Moses. The revelation of the tabernacle was first and far most a revelation of our God. It carried with it one central theme; Jesus is coming! He is the much-heralded "Seed of the Woman" that will crush the head of the serpent. In this chapter, I am not attempting to present an exhaustive study on the subject of the Tabernacle of Moses. One book would not do the subject justice, let alone one chapter. I am, however, trying to focus on what I believe is the central theme God has revealed to His people; that is, the person of Jesus Christ and His finished work. Again, everything about the Tabernacle was saying, "Jesus is coming!" So, let's take this short journey together, that we might see Him.

The message of the Tabernacle reveals Him, how He made His move toward us, and how He made known His plan for us to come in unto Him. Consider the encounter Moses had with God on the mountain. He was given instructions to build a tabernacle. The tabernacle was built for one purpose; so that God could have His dwelling place among His people. It symbolizes the various levels of spiritual maturity; as an example, Babe, Adolescence, and

Adults. This pattern is seen by the representation of the tabernacle's outer court, Holy place and Most Holy place.

"And let them make me a sanctuary; that I may dwell among them." Exodus 25:8

There is nothing unclear about our Father's heart. It is to dwell among us. The Omnipotent God longs to dwell among us! Visitation is good, but habitation, is much,

much, better. No wonder

David was overwhelmed as

he declared:

"When I think of all that you have made, the moon, sun, and the stars, what is man, that thou art mindful

of him?" Psalm 119:19

We need not question His love for us, for it has been proven before the beginning of time. Can you see the picture God has so eloquently painted for us? He made the move toward us, seeing we could not, nor did we seek to make one toward Him. The longing of His heart is now revealed. His love is being demonstrated once again. Note;

it is the Father desiring to be up close to man. Isn't it logical, that since He made the first move, He would begin revealing and unveiling from His prospective, that is, from the inside out? He began by revealing Himself by the first piece of furniture He instructed to be built, the Ark of the Testimony, or the Ark of the Covenant.

> *"And they shall make an ark of shittim[1] wood: two cubits[2] and half shall be the length thereof, and a cubit and a half the height thereof. And thou shalt overlay it with pure gold, within and without shalt thou overlay it, and shalt make upon it a crown of gold round about."* *Exodus 25:10-11*

The greater reached out or down to the lesser and the perfect to the imperfect. How humbling this is? He came out to man, that man might come in to Him. He is no longer keeping man off to a distance as it was at Mount Sinai. On Mount Sinai, God

---

[1] Shittim wood was from the acacia tree. It represents the human nature of Christ.

[2] Old unit of measurement, the length, equal to the distance from your elbow to your wrist (17-22 in)

would break forth upon man or beast if they got too close to Him. Thank God for the way home! If we remain at arm's length from Him, it is because we want to, not because we have to. Draw close to Him. He longs for it!

He commanded Moses to build the Tabernacle exactly as He described it to Him; there was no room for deviation. The reason for strict adherence was because everything about the Tabernacle was a representation of His nature. It was also a type, or foreshadowing, of Jesus Christ and His sacrificial, redemptive and sanctifying work.

> *"According to all that I show thee, after the pattern of the tabernacle, and the pattern of all the instruments thereof, even so shall ye make it."*
> *Exodus 25:9*

> *"And look that thou make them after their pattern, which was showed thee in the mount."*
> *Exodus 25:40*

As the tabernacle had to be constructed according to the word of God, so must our lives be built (lived) according to His word. There is no other way for us to come to Him. Remember this. The only program God will ever endorse is

His own, so we must establish a relationship with Him based upon the pattern (standard) already set forth in His word. We must not deviate! He wants our lives to begin, not in a form and fashion from the outside, but from the inside. A change of heart must precede a change in appearance.

The Tabernacle served as a message of hope, the hope of eternal salvation. If you and I could have had an aerial view of the completed tabernacle and the twelve tribes positioned around it, we would see a cross within a cross. Did you catch that? A cross within a cross! Even then, our God was sending a message that the enemy missed; that is, that the cross will be the launching pad from which salvation will spring forth. Can you imagine what Moses felt as he looked down upon the finished work of the tabernacle[3], and could see the cross? I can only imagine the level of joy and excitement that flooded his heart knowing

---

[3] It took 9 months to complete the tabernacle; it takes 9 months for a woman to give birth.

that the redeemer of the world was coming, and that God used him to play a role in sending the message; the message that Christ will come and liberate His people from the tyranny of sin. All the while, satan is oblivious of this plan. Aren't you glad satan is not omniscient?

God was able to communicate His plan throughout the genealogies and our enemy was always steps behind Him. Think about it? If satan understood the message God was conveying through the tabernacle, a message of the hope of the coming messiah, he would have certainly attacked without fail. As we think about the message God sent, let us also think about what God was revealing through the various furnishings. We will briefly focus on the significance of the Brazen Altar, the Brazen Laver, the Golden Candlestick, Table of Showbread and the Golden Altar of Incense.

The Brazen Altar-Salvation Begins

Upon entering the gate to the outer court of the Tabernacle, the first furnishing or instrument encountered is the Brazen Altar that was made of brass. The Brazen Altar was the only way to God and it is symbolic of the Cross of Christ, indicating that there remains but one way to the Father. The parallel is amazing; a nation had one way to God. All of the sacrifices were offered in this one place for a nation. Likewise, in our day, there is but one Altar (Cross) for the entire world, by which one can have access to God the Father. The Altar invites death as the rite of passage to the next level in the journey toward God. It certainly lives up to its meaning; to slay or slaughter.

> *"And thou shalt make an altar of shittim wood, five cubits long, and five cubits broad; the altar shall be foursquare: and the height thereof shall be three cubits. And thou shalt make the horns of it upon the four corners thereof: his horns shall be of the same: and thou shalt overlay it with brass. Exodus 27:1-2*

As the burnt offering brought life to the people in Moses' day, the Altar also reveals the fact that Christ, the perfect sacrifice, brings life to the entire world. Note: In the description of the Altar, it is referred to as "His horns." All throughout the tabernacle it consistently points to Jesus our Lord. The actions at the Altar in times past are symbolic in the believer's life today; it starts with the act of repentance. At the Altar we accept the sacrifice of the Heavenly Lamb, perfect in His offering for sin. At this point we die to our way of life. We are a new creation, born of the spirit, and salvation has begun. Notice I said, it has begun, not ended. Once the Altar experience is reality, we are propelled forward to experience the benefits of the Brazen Laver.

The Brazen Laver

"Thou shalt also make a laver of brass, and his foot (emphasis) also of brass, to wash withal: and thou shalt put it between the tabernacle of the congregation and the altar, and thou shalt put water therein. And Aaron and his sons shall wash their hands and their feet thereat. When they go into the tabernacle of the congregation, they shall wash with water, that they die not; or when they come near to the altar to minister, to burn offering made by fire unto the Lord. So they shall wash their hands and their feet, that they die not: and it shall be a statue for ever to them, even to him and to his seed throughout their generations. Exodus 30:18-21

The Brazen Laver was a large bowl made of polished brass and it was filled with water. Before I go further, I want to put emphasis on this principle; only Aaron and his sons, the priests, had access to the Laver. The Lord our God emphasized that they were to wash before ministry. This was a statue that would be forever! What does that mean to us in our day? It means that if we want to advance in the realm of the Lord, then we too must come by baptism (Laver), once and for all for the old man which is buried with Christ in baptism, as well as a daily washing to keep the new man cleansed and prepared for ministry.

Once we experience the Altar and the Laver, we move forward in our ministry as priests unto the Lord. Keep in mind, only priests were able to minister unto the Lord.

> *"But ye are a chosen generation, a royal priesthood, an holy nation, a peculiar people; that ye should shew forth the praises of him who hath called you out of darkness into his marvelous light." I Peter 2:9*

The Laver was multipurpose. As a mirror, it revealed to those approaching it their need for cleansing. The water in the laver provided the means for getting cleansed; it represented water baptism, as well as a continual cleansing. How is this principle applicable to the believer? As we look into the Word of God, it will reveal to us our need for cleansing, and it also provides us the means for cleansing. In the Apostle Paul's letter to Timothy he wrote:

> *"All scripture is given by inspiration of God (God breathed), and is profitable for doctrine, for reproof, for correction, for instruction in righteousness. That the man of God may be perfect, thoroughly furnished unto all good works."*
> *II Timothy 3:16-17*

The Lord is ever gracious in that He not only tells us what we may be doing wrong, but also shows us how to make the necessary corrections. Are you willing to look into the Word of God, and respond to what it reveals to you?

If I were to ask you, "Have you bathed today," your response would more than likely be, "Of course. What kind of question is that?" You would be correct in your response. It is silly to ask if you cleaned yourself before going to work, school, or any other activity or function. Why is it then, we give such care for washing the natural body and neglect washing from the weightier spiritual realm? It should be more ridiculous to think that we would ever leave our homes or go an entire day without bathing in His word. Let us continue to wash, that we may remain clean from the impurities of this world. As we complete each level, we have picked up another breadcrumb, growing in our maturation process.

Once we have advanced upon the pathway to God and have successfully been sacrificed and washed, then we are permitted to go into the next level of the salvation process. As we move into the Holy place (spirit-filled realm), we find three pieces of furniture; the Candle Stick, the Table of Showbread, and the Altar of incense. Each in itself represents a revelation of Christ. We will see Him as the light of the world (Candle Stick), the bread of life (Table of

Showbread), and the great High Priest (at the Altar of Incense).

The Golden Candle Stick

As the priests completed the requirements for ministry in the outercourt, they were allowed to move forward into the realm of the "Holy" place. In this realm, the priests have an encounter with light (the Golden Candlestick). The Candle Stick was made of one piece of gold with three branches on each side. Thus, revealing Jesus as the central shaft, or theme (Vine), and the church as the branches.

> *"And thou shalt make a candlestick of pure gold: of beaten work shall the candlestick be made: his shaft (emphasis), and his branches, his bowls, his knops, and his lowers, shall be of the same. And six branches shall come out of the sides of it; three branches of the candlestick out of the one side, and three branches of the candlestick out of the other side." Exodus 25:31-32*

Remember, to this point, each piece of furniture in the outercourt was made of brass, denoting the beginning of the salvation process. Much blood was shed in the realm of the outercourt. As we move in the Holy place, we enter into the spirit realm. In this realm, the material is covered with pure gold, thus, representing the divine nature of God. It is also an indication that Jesus is the light. We have no light outside of Him. We thrive because we are connected to Him. Thus, it reveals the theme of "Jesus is the Vine" (shaft of the Candlestick) and the church is the branches. When we remain connected to Him, there is no lack! Do you recall what Jesus said?

> *"I am the vine, ye are the branches. He that abideth in me, and I in him, the same bringeth forth much fruit: for without me ye can do nothing." John 15:5*

The Candle Stick provided artificial light; symbolic of He who is pure, or the divine light:

> *"Then spake Jesus again unto them, saying, I am the light of the world: he that followeth me shall not walk in darkness, but shall have the light of life." John 8:12*

Darkness represents spiritual ignorance. As long as we are in constant relationship with Jesus Christ, we WILL NOT walk in ignorance. Sad to say, in our day, many are content with the outercourt experience. They have been saved at the Altar and have gone the way of the Laver in water baptism. From the external they have the part down, a form of godliness. They carry their Bibles to service every week, but they either don't understand that there is much more to experience, or they wish to go no further in God. In many respects, they are worse off than the Ethiopian in Acts 8. Although he was confused, he was at least trying to understand. Perhaps all the traditions and various rituals of his day brought confusion when stacked up against the word he was reading? Philip happened to see him as he was passing by and noticed the Ethiopian's saddened countenance. Philip asked the Ethiopian, "What's wrong?" He replied, "I just came from worship, but I still don't understand the scriptures." What he was saying was that he did not have divine revelation, so he lacked spiritual understanding. He asked, "How can I understand, except someone shows them to me?" Philip then expounded, or shined the light of Christ upon the scriptures for him. The

Ethiopian was pierced by the truth of God's word. He responded by saying, "Now tell me, what hinders me from being baptized?

We can be Bible carrying Christians with no light; I know, because I was one of them. In order for us to move into the next dimension in God, it is necessary that we mature in the realm we are in; only then can we be propelled into the next. His light enables us to eat of Him and to go forth even farther in our walk toward Him. As this realm continues to encompass and consume us, we take the next step as priests; we sit down to eat of Him at the Table of Showbread.

The Table of Showbread

The Table of Showbread is the place where the priests sat down and ate. It was set on the opposite side of the Golden Candlestick.

"Thou shalt also make a table of shittim wood: two cubits shall be the length thereof, and a cubit the breath thereof, and a cubit and a half the height thereof. And thou shalt overlay it with pure gold, and make thereto a crown of gold round about. And thou shalt set upon the table showbread before me always." Exodus 25:23-24, 30

There is no doubt about the typology here! Jesus is the Bread of Life, and He invites us to come and eat of Him. In fact He says:

"And Jesus said unto them, I am the bread of life: he that cometh to me shall never hunger; and he that believeth on me shall never thirst." John 6:35

I thank God that this speaks to His fellowship and unlimited provision for us. We need not go without if we have made it to Him. He said that the showbread should be before Him always. Listen to me! As believers in Christ, His provision will not fail; get in position to receive of Him my friend. I declare to you this day; that if you belong to Christ, there is no lack in you, because there is no lack in

Him! We need to hold fast this truth, especially when things appear to be contrary.

Often times, when things are contrary, and we are going through what I call "a time of making," we consult with everyone about our problem. We run away from the Lord's Table, and we begin to eat from the table of our friends, saved or unsaved, coworkers, etc. We allow them to feed us and make deposits in us that did not come from the master's table. Only the diet from the Lord's Table can provide the nutrients needed to strengthen us. My friends, if you have run away from His provision, come back and sit down. It does not matter how bad things may have gotten in your life, please, come and sit down with Him! He will deliver you, and He will not perform this deliverance in secret, but rather in the open for the world to see, specifically, our adversary. The Lord wants us to have confidence in Him in the midst of the storm, to sit down and eat from Him alone.

"Thou preparest a table before me in the presence of mine enemies." Psalm 23:5

Do you know that when you and I sit down and eat from the Lord's Table when everything is chaotic, it confuses and disarms the enemy? The enemy expects us to look more on his attack than to eat from the Lord. We are nourished by the word, guided by the word, and kept by the power of His word. Each day we wake, we need to eat of Him and live. So the next time trouble comes, sit down at His table and eat! As the priests experienced the Golden Candlestick and the Table of Showbread, they were prepared, or conditioned, to move one step closer to God, by way of the Altar of Incense.

The Golden Altar of Incense

The Bible is clear as to what we enter God's presence with.

"Enter into his gates with thanksgiving; and into his courts with praise: be thankful unto him, and bless his name." Psalm 100:4

Prior to the High Priest entering into the threshold of the Holy of Holies, he was required to offer up incense that was made up of the compound God communicated to Moses. We, as believers, should take note of this one fact. The compound was mandated by God, and it was the only mixture He would accept. In Leviticus 10, Nadab and Abihu, Aaron's sons, decided they would offer God something He had not prescribed. Their error cost them their lives! As in the days of old, so it is in our day. God knows how He wants us to come before Him. We must not deviate from what He has commanded. Our praise must be from our hearts, not just lip service.

You have witnessed the salvation process by way of the tabernacle pattern. Now let's discuss what really happens to us during this process, so that we in our turn can convey the truth to someone else.

Ark of the Covenant-Mercy Seat

As the priest left the realm of praise, they entered the Holy of Holies. In this realm, the High Priest stood before the Ark of the Covenant and the Mercy Seat.

"And they shall make an ark of shittim wood: two cubits and a half shall be the length thereof, and a cubit and a half the breath thereof, and a cubic and a half the height thereof. And thou shalt overlay it with pure gold, within and without shalt thou overlay it, and shalt make a crown of gold round about.
And thou shalt make a mercy seat of pure gold: two cubits and a half shall be the length thereof, and a cubit and a half the breath thereof."
Exodus 25:10-11, 17

God told Moses that it was at this Ark of the Covenant with the Mercy Seat that He would meet him and commune with him. The Ark and everything in it represented the "Holiness of God." Inside it were the Tables of the Law, The Golden Pot of Manna and the Rod that Budded. Each of these was symbolic of a member of the Godhead. The

Mercy Seat was a lid for the Ark of the Covenant. On the Mercy Seat was sprinkled the blood of Atonement. This was done once a year by the High Priest to atone for his sins and the sins of the people. Jesus is our High Priest. He entered beyond the veil on our behalf, and in so doing, He made the way for us to access the Holy of Holies; by His blood. However, we don't have to wait a year before we can come before Him. Can you imagine having done something wrong (sin) and could not be freed from it for a whole year? That's what our ancestors endured. Jesus rent the veil, signaling that a way into the presence of God was made.

In this realm is the fullness of the spirit. This is what we would call the 100-fold realm. Jesus entered this realm as our forerunner. He is the first born of many brethren. This is the hope of the Father, that many will follow His Son in life and fellowship. However, we must understand the process of salvation so that we are not lulled to sleep; that is, thinking that we have arrived once we have an outercourt experience. There is much, much, more to experience in God. As you journey with me through the process of salvation, let me say from the outset, you may not agree with everything I have communicated, but I ask that you search the scriptures for yourself before you close your heart to it.

Salvation is a Process

As Jesus is the firstborn among many brethren, there must be a second, third, fourth, and so on. Now, I don't know what number you are. What matters most is that you are in that number of many brethren if you are born again of the spirit. I want to take the time to share with you about the salvation process, because I believe it is so misunderstood--misunderstood from the perspective of what actually happened to us once we accepted Jesus Christ as our Lord and Savior.

You see, I was always taught that upon acceptance of Jesus Christ my soul was saved. However, I have learned over the years that this may not be entirely accurate. Based upon the Tabernacle construct, it suggests a different concept all together. It tells us that salvation is a process, rather than everything happening all at once. I know this may be a position of controversy, but keep an open mind as I lay it out. Once we accepted the atonement of Christ, our spirit was reborn, or recreated. Note: Using the Tabernacle model, this takes place at the Altar. In typology, the Altar is seen as the Cross of Christ. Salvation can only begin at the cross.

Let's take a look a couple of definitions of salvation. The Greek word for salvation is "SOTERIA." It means deliverance, preservation, salvation, protection, made whole, health and safety. It emphasizes COMPLETE DELIVERANCE! The verb form is "SOZO." This word suggests a progressive work, not something that takes place all at once. The scriptures support the fact that we were born again of the spirit. Consider the following:

> *"And no man putteth new wine into old bottles: else the new doth burst the bottles, and the new wine is spilled, the bottles will be marred: but new wine MUST be put into new bottles." Mark 2:22*

Mark sets forth the same concept by the illustration of a new cloth on an old garment; and, so it is with God. In the illustration of the new wine and old bottles, the new wine represents the spirit of God. He stated that He could not put His spirit in an old vessel, or old container. Why? It would destroy it. God the Father had to create a new container. Simply put, He recreated our spirit. Our spirit has to be recreated to contain Him. You must understand that this is not the baptism of the Holy Ghost.

Let me put it this way, if you were 5'10" tall when you accepted Jesus, you were 5'10" after that. So then, nothing happened to the body. Well, how many can say to this day that you always think properly? The truth is, upon acceptance of Jesus you did not immediately begin having perfect thoughts. This is an extremely important principle to grasp. The soul is where our intellect, emotions, and our

will are housed. If I still do not think correctly one hundred percent of the time, then my soul is not yet saved. If it were, I would not need any more work done to it. Beloved, the only thing saved upon acceptance of Jesus is our spirit. Our new birth is the beginning of salvation! God's desire is to deliver the whole man.

> *"And the very God of peace sanctify you wholly; and I pray God your whole spirit and soul and body be preserved blameless unto the coming our Lord Jesus Christ." I Thessalonians 5:23*

Do you see that man must be delivered in each realm of existence; spirit, soul, and body? Man is a spirit, he possesses a soul, and he lives in a body.

> *"Who delivered us from so great a death, and doth deliver: in whom we trust that he will yet deliver us." II Corinthians 1:10*

Note the progression of tenses: delivered (past tense), doth (present tense), and yet deliver (future tense). We must ask ourselves, what has the Lord already delivered us from? If we hear the spirit, we can only conclude that He has delivered us from spiritual death only! He is delivering us (presently) in the soul realm, or if you will, the mind. As we remain faithful to His process of salvation, He will yet deliver our bodies (future).

To reiterate, we are saved, being saved, and we will be saved. My spirit is saved, my soul is being saved, and my body will be saved! There is still a work the Lord is doing and will yet do. We cannot relax and say we have arrived. That is what has happened to so many of our brothers and sisters and also why it is so difficult to convince them to change. We are spirit beings, and to tell you the truth, it should be more difficult for us to sin, than to live holy. We are after God's kind and He is Holy! He made a way for us to be with Him and like Him.

ENDNOTES/SCRIPTURES

1. Exodus 25:8-11, 40
2. Psalm 119:19
3. John 6:35
4. Psalm 23:5
5. Psalm 100:4
6. Leviticus 10
7. Mark 2:22
8. II Thessalonians 5:23
9. II Corinthians 1:10

THE HOPE OF THE CHURCH

*"And it doth not yet appear what we shall
be: but we know that, when he shall appear,
we shall be like him."*
I John 3:2-3

Believers often ask themselves what will it all mean,
living a sanctified life, and will it be worth it? The answer
is an emphatic YES! We shall be like Him! It may not feel
or look like it will ever happen, but I assure you by the
word of the Lord, it will! He has taken too many steps and
made too many promises for it not to happen. When we
were lost, without hope, God took action because He

believed we were worth saving. He did not hesitate to send the best gift heaven had to offer, His son Jesus! He did so in the hope that many would accept His gift and live. Once we have accepted Jesus Christ, we begin a lifelong journey of becoming like Christ. Our Father begins making us over again. He told the prophet Jeremiah to go down to the potter's house, and there he would hear the words of the Lord:

> *"Then I went down to the potter's house, and, behold, he wrought a work on the wheels. And the vessel that he made of clay was marred in the hand of the potter: so he made it again another vessel, as seemed good to the potter to make it." Jeremiah 18:3-4*

I like how The Message Bible puts it, that when the pot turned out badly, the potter would simply start all over again using the same clay to make another pot. We all were born and shaped in iniquity. God loved us so much, He was not going to leave us that way. He made provision for us that we might be made into another vessel. Only, this time, according to the apostle Paul in I Corinthians 15:45, the pattern changed, from the first Adam (living soul) to the second Adam, Jesus Christ (quickening spirit). Through Jesus Christ we are now quickened in the spirit, that we might live as He lived. The Father is clear as He communicated this truth through the apostle Paul.

> *"For whom he did foreknow, he also did predestinate to be conformed to the image of his Son, that he might be the firstborn among many brethren. Romans 8:29*

> *"God knew what he was doing from the very beginning. He decided from the outset to shape the lives of those who love him along the same lines as the life of his Son. The Son stands first in the line of humanity he restored. We see the original and intended shape of our lives there in him."*
> *Romans 8:29 (The Message Bible)*

Is this not powerful? Our lives are shaped to that of His Son Jesus Christ! God intends for us to carry out our lives as Jesus did. Jesus proved that we could live a victorious life in the flesh. Now it is time for us to believe that we can go through this life victorious, without loss.

Refuse to Lose

I often say I will never lose again the rest of my life.

Many think I am boasting in my position and ability, but on the contrary, I boast in the Father and the promises we have in Jesus Christ. Why settle for losing when our forerunner has proven otherwise? How long my brother or sister will you be content with losing? Decide to stop today. You can! I have discovered over the years through my own life experiences that when one is content with losing, he or she will find ways to accommodate it. I don't believe our Father can get glory out of our lives when we lose all the time and at everything. In fact, I don't believe we can afford to lose, period!

Consider what Rahab said to the spies Joshua sent into Jericho:

> *"And she said unto the men, I know that the Lord hath given you the land, and that your terror is fallen upon us, and that all the inhabitants of the land faint because of you. For we have heard how the Lord dried up the water of the Red Sea for you, when ye came out of Egypt; and what ye did unto the two kings of the Amorites, that were on the other side Jordan, Sihon, and Og, whom ye utterly destroyed. And as soon as we had heard these things, our hearts did melt, neither did there remain*

any more courage in any man, because of you: for the Lord your God, he is God in heaven above, and in the earth beneath."
Joshua 2:9-11

We need to be in a position to allow God to move through our lives, and when He does, the enemy will hear about it. The enemy heard how God moved on behalf of His people in Joshua's day, and as a result, all their courage was gone. God changes not! This can happen in our day. It can happen to you if you position yourself for it. The Lord stands ready to release His strength on our behalf!

It will take a people whose hearts are perfect toward Him. He will not release all that He is for us in the public arena until we have given Him control of our lives in the private arena. However, when He has seen a commitment from us in private, He will begin moving, flexing His spiritual muscles, and it will send ripples of fear in the heart of our enemy. We cannot afford to lose! Stop accommodating it; get in position and start declaring what the Lord has spoken over you, that is, that He has made you like Jesus, more than a conqueror. Jesus conquered all! He is now, Lord of Lords, King of Kings.

Decide today to stop declaring that you are not worth what the Father did for you. What do I mean by that? I hear continually, born again believers confessing and singing, "I am so unworthy." In fact, I use to say and sing the same melodies myself. However, I have learned that perhaps it is not a wise thing to question God's decision-making prowess. I have to ask, are we really qualified to question what God says or does? He thought we were worth saving, so let us not debate His wisdom. His desire is that we live and be like His firstborn son. My brothers and sisters, it does not matter what we have encountered in this life. No matter how difficult the season we are living in, our hope should be in the fact that God is using all these things to shape us, and in the end, we will look and act like our elder brother, Jesus Christ. Let us consider this point from God's prospective and maybe His hope will become our hope.

The Seed and the Harvest

Let us begin with a very basic example. Having grown up exposed to farming, when we planted seed in the ground, we did so in the hope that what went into the ground would yield offspring just like it. If a watermelon seed went into the ground, we expected watermelons to come forth from the seed. This is an important principle to hold on to as we look into, and attempt to understand, what our heavenly Father is also looking for. Ask yourself, what did God plant? He planted His son Jesus in the earth.

> *"Verily, verily, I say unto you, Except a corn of wheat fall into the ground and die, it abideth alone: but if it die, it bringeth forth much fruit."*
> *John 12:24*

Notice that John says except it falls into the ground. This presupposes a yielding, no fight or struggle. Jesus is the seed that God planted into the heart of the earth, and He did so with one purpose in mind, to bring many sons to glory. God the Father wants us to look like the seed He planted; He wants us to look like Jesus. Beloved, He will not accept anything less. He does not want us to look like Paul, Peter, James, nor John. These were all great men of the faith, but they were not the perfect sacrifice for sin. He wants us to look like JESUS! Do you remember the transfiguration scene? When Jesus was transfigured, Peter, James, and John were able to witness this moment. The spirit of God overshadowed them, enabling them to endure the moment. Then Peter said, "It is good for us to be here. Let us build three tabernacles, one for Moses, Elijah and Jesus." After hearing what Peter had to say, God responded with an emphatic *no*! Matthew recorded the event saying:

"While he (Peter) yet spake, behold, a bright cloud

overshadowed them: and behold, a voice out of the cloud, which said, This is my beloved Son, in whom I am well pleased; hear ye him." Matthew 17:5

God was being very clear to Peter, emphasizing the need for Peter and the others to hear Jesus, and that that was where their focus should be rather than on Moses and Elijah. As Jesus is the hope of the church, being like Him is the mandate of the Father. We are not to model our lives after our pastors; however, we are to follow them as they follow Christ. Understanding this fact will help us understand why the Father will not accept anyone at His table that does not resemble the Son. There are no short cuts!

I have shared with you the mandate of our Father. It is not to have more services and functions, so steer clear from much serving for the sake of serving. All that we do should be out of love and obedience to our Lord. Keep in mind, it is not the functions or services that make us holy; it is our hearing the word and obeying it. It is our being set apart for

His use. That being said, do not measure yourself or anyone else based upon the number of services you attend.

As we grow in our obedience to the Lord, we understand more fully why we need to hear His voice. I hear quite frequently in various church venues that we are forever working for the Lord. While I understand what most mean by it, it is not an accurate declaration. We are not working for the Lord; we are workers together with Him. The message to the church in Corinth addressed this issue saying:

"We then, as workers together with him, beseech you also that ye receive not the grace of God in vain." II Corinthians 6:1

As companions in His work, let us not squander the gift He has given us by much serving, but never actually   hearing His words. Consider Martha and Mary at this   juncture in their lives. Jesus has come to their house. He has something to say, yet each of them had a different focus; one focused on serving, while the other, gazed upon His face. Jesus commented on the choices they made. The difference, He said, had to do with what could and could not be taken. Mary chose that good part that would never be taken away.

Will you gaze long enough into the face of the Lord? I am not talking about taking a glance, but gazing into His face long enough to be changed? To gaze means to look steadily upon. It presupposes that one must do this without distraction. That's the challenge before us all. Will we do like Mary, and sit at His feet as long as He is speaking? What happens to us when we look upon him steadfastly? Consider for a moment why the face is important. The face is that part of our human body which contains a person's unique characteristics. David declared this:

> *"As for me, I will behold thy face in righteousness: I shall be satisfied, when I awake, with thy likeness." Psalm 17:15*

> *"And me? I plan on looking you full in the face. When I get up, I'll see your full stature and live*

heaven on earth." Psalm 17:15 The Message Bible

David understood the transforming power the Lord has upon them that look upon Him. We take on His characteristics and His attributes when we gaze. We bring heaven to earth.

If I Be Lifted Up

I am reminded of a message I preached entitled, "Bitten by the Serpent." The focus of the message was not on the serpent, but rather on looking upon Jesus. Jesus declared:

> *"And as Moses lifted up the serpent in the wilderness, even so must the Son of man be lifted up. That whosoever believeth in him should not perish, but have eternal life." John 3:14-15*

Jesus drew on an analogy between His cross and the bronze (brass) snake Moses raised on a pole. As you recall, the people murmured against God and Moses for their wilderness experience. They had flashbacks of being in Egypt where they, in their minds, had enjoyed an ample supply bread and water. Oh! How quickly we get rocked to sleep. They focused more on their provision in Egypt more than the slavery. Is this you today? Have you focused more on the provision, what you have, rather than the slavery that it brings? Well, God responded to their complaint by sending fiery serpents among them. Many died as a result. The people repented, as it was their custom to do after God's anger was kindle against them. God commanded Moses:

> *"And the Lord said unto Moses, make thee a fiery serpent, and set it upon a pole: and it shall come to pass, that every one that is bitten, when he looketh upon it, shall live. And Moses made a serpent of brass, and put it upon a pole, and it came to pass, that if a serpent had bitten any man, when he beheld the serpent of brass, he lived." Numbers 21:8-9*

I want to point out that the people were never bitten until they got out of the will of God. Meaning, when they complained against God and His servant, they got outside His will. In fact, the apostle Paul reminds us in the Book of Colossians, that our life is hid in Christ with God. So the only way the enemy can get to us is when come out of God. Jesus said He would be lifted up as the serpent and He has been. He was lifted up on the cross, and in so doing, He became sin for us, that we might be made the righteousness of God in Him. We are now in Him! Jesus became the curse for us! Our sins were transferred on Him, and all we need do to receive from His act of grace, is gaze upon Him. This sounds like a simple thing, but many struggle to look upon Him.

In the natural realm, there are many different species of snakes on the planet (approximately 2700). Of all of them, only about 300 are considered poisonous. Each poisonous snake carries venom that is either Hemotoxic or Neurotoxic. That is, it will either attack the blood or nervous system. Whenever an individual is bitten, they are always asked if they saw what type of snake it was that bit them. Why is this important? They need to know what type of antivenin to administer. Likewise, we are confronted with various levels of the enemy's hierarchy, and we need to know what we are dealing with. Consider what Ephesians reveals:

> *"For we wrestle not against flesh and blood, but against principalities, against powers, against the rulers of the darkness of this world, against spiritual wickedness in high places." Ephesians 6:12*

Do you remember when the disciples came to Jesus telling Him that they could not cast a demon out of this individual? Jesus told them, **"This kind** only goes out by prayer and fasting." Our adversary has many waiting on the opportunity to inject us with

his venom of lust, lying, covetousness, unforgiveness, etc. In the natural realm, once a person is bitten, the 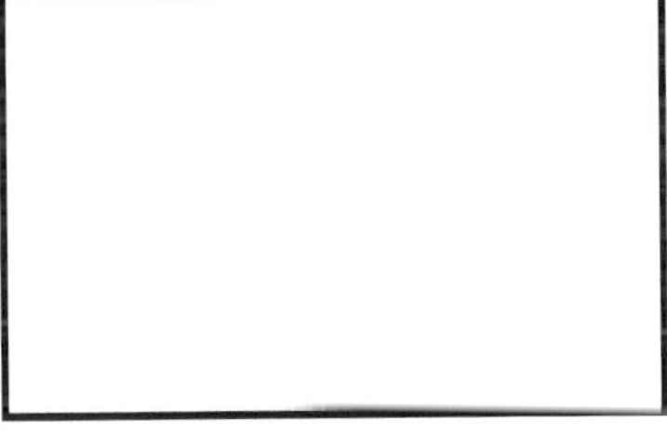 evidence of it is quickly apparent. There is swelling, extreme pain, burning, shortness of breath, and so on. Beloved, just as these symptoms cannot be hidden; so it is in the spirit. Many are walking around with evidence in their lives that they have been bitten by the serpent, yet, they refuse to look upon the Lord Jesus Christ for healing. As the antivenin was the only remedy for healing, so, too, is Jesus the only remedy for the serpent's bite of sin. Understand this; everyone must gaze upon the Lord for themselves. We cannot rely on dad or mom's faith to save us; we must   undertake this step in faith alone.

Many are waiting to see Him in us. The man said, "Sir, I would see Jesus!" Let us do what is required to reveal Jesus to those that look for Him. There are many facets His face represents, and they are relevant to us today. Ezekiel said He has the face of a man, a lion, an ox, and an eagle. The face of a man reveals Jesus as the Son of man, the face of a lion reveals Him as the King of kings, the face of an ox reveals Him as the servant of the Most High God and the face of the eagle reveals Him as the resurrected Son of God. Praise and Glory be unto Him forever! God has chosen and entrusted us to reveal Jesus in His fullness in these four areas to this world. In fact, in the Book of Romans, the apostle reminds us that the creation is on tiptoes, waiting for the manifestation of the sons of God. They are waiting for us to come into view, and when we do, the world will see Him, in whose face we have gazed. We will then go forth to our particular assignments with assurance of victory. I do not believe there is a nobler calling than to be like Jesus. But understand something my dear brothers and sisters, this will not happen without the fire.

The Baptism of Fire

I want to illustrate how important the fire is to our growth in Christ by the process of baking a cake. As a kid I was so excited when mom told us she was going to bake a chocolate cake, my favorite by the way. I was excited because after she finished with the mixing bowl, we all had a chance to lick the bowl and the utensils clean. Well, I watched my mom put the ingredients in a bowl: flour, oils, eggs, sugar, etc. After she mixed all the ingredients together, she put the mixture in cake pans. The mixture was ready for the final stage needed to bring it to completion; the mixture needed the heat. Now I ask you, was it a cake before she put it in the oven? The answer to this question may vary. I firmly believe it was a cake before my mom put it in the oven. Everything was already in it! It simply needs the heat of the oven to bring it to its final form. Likewise, if we have Jesus Christ in us, we, too, are like

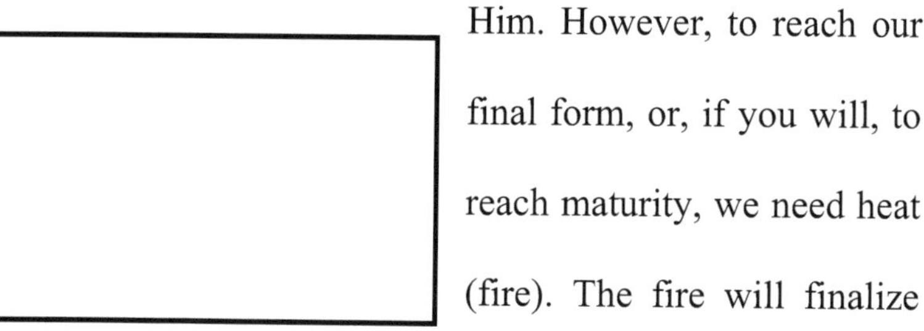 Him. However, to reach our final form, or, if you will, to reach maturity, we need heat (fire). The fire will finalize our transformation; we will look and act just like Jesus.

As we go through the maturation process, it is good to understand what transpires as we are going through the fire, and what position our Father has taken while we are in it.

Let us consider what the Lord spoke through Malachi:

"And he shall sit as a refiner and purifier of silver: and he shall purify the sons of Levi, and purge them as gold and silver, that they may offer unto the Lord an offering in righteousness." Malachi 3:3

Wow! He said that He would sit, that means He will take time with the sons of Levi; to ensure they offer Him an offering in righteousness. Remember, the sons of Levi were priests. We are that royal priesthood that the Lord is sitting in the midst of. Hallelujah! I don't know about you, but this is a message of hope. We will get there! If there are any doubts that suggest we will never get to the place He speaks of, throw it all out. Prepare yourself for the fire!!!

I am reminded of a story I heard years ago. A group of women met for a time of study in the word. Their topic for study was Malachi, Chapter 3. As they read about God sitting among the sons of Levi as a refiner of silver, one of the women asked how silver was actually purified. Well, they all were curious about it, so they sought out to find someone that actually did this sort of thing; that way, they would have firsthand knowledge of the process. In their search, they finally found an old gentleman that purified silver. He agreed to give them a demonstration and answer any questions they might have. When they arrived at the old man's shop, he provided them with the safety gear required to tour his shop. He then picked up a set of tongs and walked over to the bin where raw silver was kept. He picked up a piece and walked over to the furnace. He opened the slot provided and placed the silver in the middle of the flame. One of the women asked him, "Why did you put the silver in the middle of the flame?" He answered, "Because that's where the fire is the hottest." He sat there watching through a glass intently at the silver.

Another woman asked him if he was going to sit there the whole time to watch it? He replied, "I have to. You see, if the silver were left for a moment longer than it should be, it would be ruined." Aren't you glad the Lord watches over us without slumber?

Finally, another woman asked, "How do you know when the silver is ready?" He looked at her with a smile on his face, and said, "When I can see my reflection in it." That's exactly what the Lord wants from His people. He must send us through the fire and He will do it until He can see His reflection in us. Remember I said that He is looking for the seed he planted and His name is Jesus. Do not be afraid of the fire; welcome it, because it will be the catalyst for bringing us to the place where we walk as did our elder brother.

ENDNOTES/SCRIPTURES

1. I John 3:2-3
2. Jeremiah 18:3-4
3. I Corinthians 15:45
4. Romans 8:29
5. The Message Bible
6. Joshua 2:9-11
7. John 12:24
8. Matthew 17:5
9. Psalm 17:15
10. John 3:14-15
11. Numbers 21:8-9
12. Ephesians 6:12

13. Malachi 3:3

5

KINGDOM INFLUENCE

"Ye are the salt of the earth...Ye are the light of the world." Matthew 5:13-14

As I travel locally and abroad, I am saddened by the condition of the various communities I visit. Why? I see communities absent of light and not properly seasoned with salt. How can this be? In some communities, it seems like local church buildings are on every other corner. The Lord ministered to me about this, and I have repeated this wherever I go. If the church is in a community and that community is dying, the church needs to be asking, why?

We were called by the Lord to be agents of change. He deposited the church in the community of His choosing to be the difference.

We cannot sit around and complain about how bad things are; we must add our influence and produce the change we want to see. We are more than capable of achieving this level of influence because Jesus has already done it. He is the pattern set before us; therefore, we are left without excuses. The two agents of change the Lord used to describe the church are salt and light.

> *"Ye are the salt of the earth: but if the salt has lost his savor, wherewith shall it be salted? It is thenceforth good for nothing, but to be cast out, and to be trodden under foot of men. Ye are the light of the world. A city that is set on a hill cannot be hid. Neither do men light a candle, and put it under a bushel, but on a candlestick; and it giveth light unto all that are in the house. Let your light so shine before men, that they may see your good works, and glorify your Father which is in heaven."*
> *Matthew 5:13-16*

Now please indulge me and read the same scriptures in their entirety from The Message Bible translation. I think it hits the mark where emphasis is required.

> *"Let me tell you why you are here. You're here to be salt-seasoning that brings out the God-flavors of this earth. If you lose your saltiness, how will people taste godliness? You've lost your usefulness and will end up in the garbage. Here's another way to put it: You're here to be light, bring out the God-colors in the world. God is not a secret to be kept. We're going public with this, as public as a city on a hill. If I make you light bearers, you don't think I'm going to hide you under a bucket, do you? I'm putting you on a light stand. Now that I've put you there on a hilltop, on a light stand-shine! Keep open house; be generous with your lives. By opening up to others, you'll prompt people to open up with God, this generous Father in heaven."*
> *Matthew 5:13-16 (The Message Bible)*

Beloved, can you see how influential we are in Christ? We are His agents of change! As you well know, salt seasons, preserves, freshens, sweetens, creates thirst, and when needed, it combats and melts ice. He has sent us to bring this type of influence to dead or dying people, communities, towns, cities, and nations. He sent us, the church of the Lord Jesus Christ, not the government. Please don't misunderstand me; I am not speaking against government in any form. The government has its role in

God's plan, but it is not to free people from sin.

We, the Church, are called to free men and women from the grip of satan and tyranny of sin. We are to show the entire world they can live a holy and joyful life before the only true God and reap the benefits of His favor. Let us not complain about the environment in which we live, work and socialize. As His agents of change, change the environment by your presence.

Stay Salty

I must point out that we will not maximize our potential if we are not right before God in private. We must allow God to plow our lives, thus, making us meet to plow. Then we can make salt deposits in the lives of others. Once we are able to make salt deposits in the lives of others, we must not become relaxed in our relationship with the Lord.

We need to remain ever vigilant and dependent upon

Him, so that we do not lose our edge, or our ability to continue making deposits in those around us. Always remember, it is God that has made us salty, and it is God that is able to help us maintain our saltiness.

If we have lost our saltiness, how will people be able to taste godliness? In the Old Testament, we find in the Book of Leviticus, beginning in Chapter Two, if a sacrifice was brought to the Altar without salt, it was considered not prepared for God's acceptance. Wow! It was not ready for God to receive it. Are you prepared for God to receive you? If you are not, don't you think it is time to get in position where you will be acceptable to Him? How much longer will you try skirting around God's standard for your life? You have tried everything else, isn't it now time to try His way? He loves you and wants to free you, not just for yourself, but for all those within your circle. You see, until one is out of the ditch, how can he or she possibly know how to help another out. Let God have you today! Become as the   apostle Paul says to the church in Rome:

"I beseech you therefore, brethren, by the mercies of God, that ye present your bodies a living sacrifice, holy, acceptable unto god, which is your reasonable service." Romans 12:1

The disciples were God's salt to the world. They continued to sprinkle humanity with the salt from heaven. They are gone and now we are God's salt. When was the last time you sprinkled yourself on someone else? Always remember my beloved, the only way a sacrifice is acceptable unto God is that it is sprinkled with salt and that the saltiness remains.

You Are Light, So Shine!

Jesus said that we are also light. Light is meant to shine, give direction, and it gives off warmth. As light, we are to radiate and point others in the right direction. I like how The Message Bible puts it, that we are here to bring out the God-colors in the world. Our belief in Christ is not something to keep a secret. What do you mean? Many today do not want people to know that they are Christians.

They do not show forth any light because they are afraid of the criticisms that might follow. They do not take a stand in public on anything, especially if the world sees the issue as controversial.

I don't suggest that we must be heard all the time; on the contrary, I believe our faith in Christ should be as evident as a city on the top of a hill. We should be readily seen by our walk. This is what Jesus compared our influence to. We may not say a word, but our connection to Jesus Christ should be apparent from a distance. But this does not give us a pass; we must be heard at the appointed times. We should be a voice to be reckoned with in the earth.

The evidence is readily apparent for those walking in the light. You can be around a person for a few minutes and sense they have spent time with God. They will never have to say a word; their light is evident, and it radiates and touches everyone around them. Can you relate? We are called to be light-bearers. Don't shrink back because you might be rejected.

When the former president of South Africa, Nelson Mandela, addressed a nation, he stated that it was not their darkness they feared, but rather their light. He said their shrinking back did not serve the world. I believe he recognized the fact that being light would bring a scrutiny many would not wish to be exposed to. However, we are called to give ourselves away, that others might live. In fact, the apostle Paul reminds us of this principle:

> *"As it is written, For thy sake we are killed all the day long; we are accounted as sheep for the slaughter."* Romans 8:36

It should not be a surprise to us that fiery trials come our way. They come precisely because we are light. Let us not forget, there will always be enmity between the seed of the woman and satan's offspring. The world will never be a friend of our God; therefore, it will never be our friend. We must arm ourselves as children of light to fulfill the mandate that is upon us, regardless of the resistance and rejection we face. Will you make the choice to let your light shine?

ENDNOTES/SCRIPTURES

1. Matthew 5:13-16
2. The Message Bible
3. Leviticus 2
4. Romans 12:1
5. Romans 8:36

THE CALL TO REPRODUCE

"And her adversary also provoked her sore, for to make her fret, because the Lord had shut up her womb." I Samuel 1:6

In this chapter I will share with you what it means to reproduce, or, if you will, to be impregnated with God's purpose for one's life. I will highlight why it is so vitally important for us to reproduce, and secondly, the characteristics or habits of those impregnated for reproduction.

To be able to reproduce means that you have been impregnated by God to fulfill His purpose for your life and for the lives of others. It means you are a person of vision; without it, you would not have the spiritual discipline to endure the term of pregnancy. Many have committed spiritual abortion because of a lack of vision. Let me make this point; God will not impregnate anyone against their will. You and I must agree to carry His seed. Consider for a moment what happened during what is known as "The Immaculate Conception."

> *"And the angel said unto her, Fear not, Mary: for thou hast found favor with God. And, behold, thou shalt conceive in thy womb, and bring forth a son, and shalt call his name Jesus. And Mary said, Behold the handmaid of the Lord; be it unto me according to thy word." Luke 1:30-31, 38*

Note: Mary was presented with the Lord's purpose and vision for her life. She caught the vision, she agreed with God, and was therefore a partner with the Lord in His plan. Her agreement allowed God to move on the scene legally; that is, He impregnated her with His seed, and came to the earth in bodily form. As John declared unto us, "The Word was made flesh."

Hannah's Plight

Early on I mentioned Hannah's plight. What was it? It was the mere fact that her enemy looked at her with contempt because she was barren. Peninnah provoked Hannah to the point of utter dismay. It is also the same for every believer who is and has been barren. As I mentioned early on in this book, we cannot afford to lose, neither can we allow this type of behavior from our enemy to continue. There's no greater joy for our adversary the devil, than to see born again believers barren of God's purpose. This is why we must reproduce. Let us take a deeper look into Hannah's plight and draw from her experience.

We find that Hannah had been a faithful church worshipper, that is, she went up with Elkanah her husband every year to Shiloh to worship; yet, her enemy tormented her every year for being barren. She realized the only way to rid herself of the enemy was to reproduce. To do that, she knew she had to change how she approached the Father. After she worshipped with Elkanah, she decided to go and worship the Father on her own. You need to understand how dangerous this was for her. The Philistines were in the land and this made any travel dangerous. Yet, she was determined to get God's attention.

Oh, dear brothers and sisters, perhaps you, too, have been living a lie. Maybe you have been faithful attending church services and functions, but in private the enemy has been having his way with you. In other words, you look good, but you are still losing in this life. I believe the battle is won in the private arena. That is, we make a conscious choice to walk before God in private where nobody else can see. When our heart is to do it this way, we are not concerned with recognition; neither are we looking for the accolades from man. All we want is Him. This approach will get His   attention, and then He will begin to show forth His strength through our lives in public; and as a result of His   manifested strength, other lives will be forever changed.

When Hannah changed her approach to God in private, she was changed. Note: When God changes us, it also has a profound impact on our enemy! Hannah went before God alone and poured her heart out before Him; after which, her actions revealed that she believed God heard her cry. You see, when we have approached God in faith, our actions will correspond. Consider her actions:

> *"And she said, let thine handmaid find grace in thy sight. So the woman went her way, and did eat, and her countenance was no more sad."*
> *I Samuel 1:18*

I want to reiterate that Hannah was provoked by her adversary year after year. The adversary's goal was to make Hannah fret, or to be of a sad countenance. Well, it was working; she was miserable. No matter how much her husband loved her and lavished her with gifts, Hannah was still sad. Yet, we read that after Hannah poured out her soul 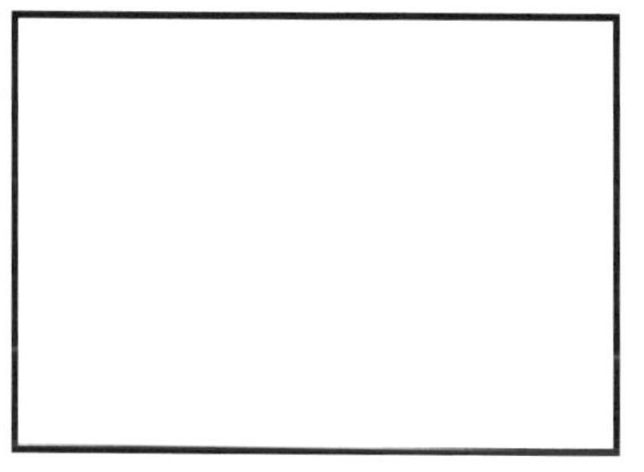 to God, she got up and did eat and her countenance was no more sad. Why was she able to overcome such sadness? Because when Hannah got up from praying, by faith she was already pregnant. She carried herself as a pregnant woman.

How does this relate to the believer today? She believed she was pregnant when she got up and she carried herself as such. As believers in Christ, when we come before God, whatever we ask of Him in faith, we receive it the moment we ask for it. From that moment, we must carry ourselves as a people pregnant with the Lord's purpose. In the natural, women who find out they are pregnant change their behavior. We must do the same when we pray to God. We must arise and live like we believe we are impregnated with His purpose.

Once a woman finds out she is expecting a child, she makes necessary changes in her life to protect the life that is in her. She will not do the things she did before pregnancy if it puts her and the child at risk. Likewise, we, too, must carry ourselves differently when we have conceived by God. Our focus must be to protect the life that is in us. That means we reevaluate how we carried ourselves before we were impregnated and make the necessary adjustments to ensure we do not jeopardize the seed of God we carry. It might mean that we cut off a few friends, remove ourselves from the party scene, and much more. Hosea says that without a vision, people perish; they cast off restraint. They do what they want to do. Lack of vision will give way to this behavior.

As pregnant people seem to have a sense for recognizing other pregnant people when no one else can, it is also true from the spiritual perspective. If you are pregnant with vision, you can easily tell those around you that are also pregnant. You see, even in the natural, if a woman is pregnant, she can't help but start showing it. Her body will undergo many physical changes she can not control. Her body does this so it can prepare for the birth of the baby. We, too, when spiritually impregnated with vision, will go through various changes to make sure we are prepared to deliver the baby (vision) in us. As a result of Hannah's change, the enemy lost his power over her and could no longer provoke her. Even so it is with us.

I had reached a similar point in my life. Just as Hannah was prior to changing her approach to God, I was also attending worship services. In fact, I was very active in the church, but to be brutally honest, I was unfruitful. I was unfruitful because the devil was having his way with me in private. I was not victorious in anything. That's right, I lived a double life. In II Timothy 3:5 the apostle Paul described me perfectly, "Having a form of godliness, but denying the power thereof: from such turn away."

Beloved, I lived a lie! One day, it seemed like everything came crumbling down upon my head. My sin against the Lord impacted not just me, but others as well. Sin has what I call the "Ripple Effect." Have you ever taken a rock or pebble and dropped it in a small pond or in any body of water? What happens? Ripples of water head out in every direction. I equate the ripples to the impact sin has in our lives. Lives are crippled in every direction, and more importantly, those affected by our sin also end up with a damaged view of our God.

I played the harlot in the street, while at the same time, I played the role of a clean and polished servant in front of people. Many families were impaired because I yielded to the spirit of lust. My actions were selfish in nature. I was deceived in my thinking; that is, thinking that I should have and do whatever I wanted. I had become what I most feared; a castaway. The Apostle Paul left on record the results of an undisciplined life to the Church at Corinth:

"I therefore run, not as uncertainly; so fight I, not as one that beateth the air: But I keep under my body, and bring it into subjection: lest that by any means, when I have preached to others, I myself should be a castaway." I Corinthians 9:26-27

The Message Bible describes this as a person caught napping. Well, I was caught napping. My behavior indicated a man without vision. I will elaborate more on this when I talk about the prodigal son. A person without a vision is DANGEROUS!

Let me say this to those of you who would defend your behavior because you do some good things along the way. We can be in sin, do some good things, and people benefit from them. But make no mistake; none of those good things and activities will ever profit you in your walk with the Lord. All good things are not necessarily God things. All the good things done during my time of napping did not profit me at all in my walk with the Lord. He wanted my heart, but my heart was still on loan to selfishness. I did not want to break from my circle of friends and WORLDLY activities. As I reflect on that time and the impact it had, it grieves my heart and I say even in tears, beloved, change your mind before many are misled and many are hurt by your actions. I know that if you identified with anything I have written about being a castaway, you are miserable! I know this, because I lived it myself. There is no true peace in your heart. Be honest with yourself; when our lives in private are steep in sin, we cannot   reproduce, and as a result, we will continue to bare the reproach of the enemy. Don't you want to change things? Then, do what I did; repent before God quickly and commit to His way only.

I feel obligated to let you know that just because you repent, it does not mean that you will not encounter the discipline of the Lord. In fact, the Bible is clear that He chastens those He loves. I understand more intimately why the Apostle encouraged us to endure the chastening of the Lord because it does not feel good, but it does cure what ails us. I pray that my experience be an encouragement to you as you take the necessary steps toward God in repentance and faith.

I remember when life took a turn for me years ago. Where things used to be easy, difficulty began to rear its head. It seemed like everything became extremely hard for me. And when my finances were affected, it really awakened me from the nap I had been taking for so long. Beloved, I could not pay my bills and I could barely keep food in the house. The phrase "too broke to pay attention" was my reality. So I did what most would have done; I got another job. I thought that the additional job would supplement where I was lacking. No matter how much I worked, nothing changed. In fact, things got worse!

Do you remember I stated that sin has a ripple effect? Well, what was happening to me was impacting my wife. It grieved me to see that my sin had now touched someone who was totally innocent of any wrongdoing. The hand of the Lord was manifesting upon me, as a loving Father. He was squeezing me and everything about me.

As things around me were being squeezed, I could not understand why. I asked myself time and time again, "Why are things getting so bad? I mean, after all, I repented for my sins, shouldn't things be getting better?" I was at a place where I could not pay my house payment, car payment, and every other payment. Have you ever been there? The time had come when I got the old eviction notice (foreclosure) for the house. And in the midst of this, I walked out one morning to get in my truck, and it wasn't there. Mr. Repo Man had paid me a courtesy visit through the night. I walked back in the house, told my wife what had happened, sat down in amazement, or better yet, bewilderment. It seemed I was being forced into a place I did not want to acknowledge or be a part of.

My wife shared with me that the only way out was to file bankruptcy. I could not conceive this, so I quickly rejected it. I figured, all I needed to do was to get another job; NOT! Another job did not cut it. It appeared to me that the more I worked, the more I lost. We had to get out of the house pretty quickly, so I asked my mother-in-law if we could stay with her until I found a place. Beloved, I can't tell you how much this hurt. I felt inadequate as a husband, father, and provider. I made a promise to my mother-in-law that I would take care of her daughter and now I was bringing her back home. My mother-in-law never said a word to me, but I knew she was disappointed by how I was taking care of her daughter.

After I moved Tonja and my daughter Arianna in, I remember having to go back to the house to finish cleaning up before the doors were closed on it for good. Not a sound was in the house, except this annoying beep from the smoke detectors. I broke down that night before God and I remember saying to Him, "Lord, if you deliver me, I will serve you for the rest of my life." My brothers and sisters, I made a decision in private that I would surrender to the hand of the Lord. I did! And even though I lost everything, I knew God heard me, and I knew within my heart that a new day had dawned.

God is faithful! We had stayed with my mother-in-law for about a week or so when God's favor was manifested. While my wife was out looking for a place for us to live, the Lord led her to this townhouse complex. When she arrived, she realized she had been by there before, but there were no vacancies. However, on this day, a sign was just put outside. Tonja arranged a time for us to see it, and we did. I told the gentleman that day that I had recently filed bankruptcy, and my wife chimed in with some powerful words. I remember her telling the gentleman, "If you give us the opportunity to move in, I promise, we will pay you all and make sure we do it on time." Her words were filled with power. I then shared with the gentleman all we had been through. He said to me, "I am grateful that you shared with me about your plight and the bankruptcy." He stated that he would have the key ready for us shortly. My wife and I rejoiced because we both knew this gentleman was a manifestation of God's grace to us.

My dear brothers and sisters, in a matter of two to three years God had restored all that we had ever lost; house, car, money, etc. He performed to me what He promised through His servant Joel, that He would restore the years that were taken. He will do the same for you, but He wants your heart to belong to Him alone. He wants you to be His in private.

> *"And I will restore to you the years that the locust hath eaten, the cankerworm, and the caterpillar, and the palmerworm, my great army which I sent among you. And ye shall eat in plenty, and be satisfied, and praise the name of the Lord your God, that hath dealt wondrously with you: and my people shall never be ashamed." Joel 2:25-26*

I knew after going through all of that, God was about to do something in my life and the life of my family. He had to make sure I did not abort what He wanted to do. And I knew in my heart that I would no longer be unfruitful. Just as Hannah knew the pain of being unfruitful, I experienced it as well. Just as she learned the joy of reproducing; I knew I would learn this as well. You can too my brothers and sisters. Repent! No flesh will ever glory in His presence. Our private lives must change if we are going to reproduce.

As you recall, I said I was not reproducing because of my lifestyle. Well, after the dealings of the Lord, He orchestrated a move in my life that I could not have foreseen. I was serving as a Professor at the Roanoke Theological Seminary, and on this particular day, I dismissed class. Well, there was a lady that lingered behind, Barbara Walton. I remember telling her that class was dismissed. She replied, "Dr. Fisher, we need you to come to our church and teach what you taught today." She told me where her church was, in Hobbsville, North Carolina. Hobbsville. Really! I had no idea where Hobbsville was at the time and did not care to know. I had my sight on something bigger and better, at least that was what I told myself. Well, I could not shake her words; it was as if it was a Macedonia Cry! I agreed to meet with the church leadership. Well, since I knew not where Hobbsville was, I did what most folk do today; I googled it! My wife and I decided to see if we could find the place a day or so before the meeting. After riding for about 20 minutes or so, my wife and I said, how far is this place? We thought we would never get there. Well, we finally did, and my wife said, "This is where the Lord is going to plant us." She was excited about it; I, however, was saying to myself, I know the Lord did not bring us way down here to this small place. I remember questioning it time and time again, and then I heard the Lord speak to me saying, "This is the place, like a root out of dry ground, I will breathe life in this place, and it shall be a beacon of light and hope." You see, God knew the soil I needed to be planted in to fulfill His purpose. I submitted to the will of God and became the Senior Pastor of Blanchard's Grove Missionary Baptist Church.

No matter what I had achieved in life in the natural realm, it didn't mount up to a hill of beans. I know by experience now what the Apostle Paul meant when he said:

"Yea doubtless, and I count all things but loss for the excellency of the knowledge of Christ Jesus my Lord: for whom I have suffered the loss of all things, and do count them but dung, that I may win Christ. And be found in him, not having mine own righteousness, which is of the law, but that which is through the faith of Christ, the righteousness which is of God by faith."
Philippians 3:8-9

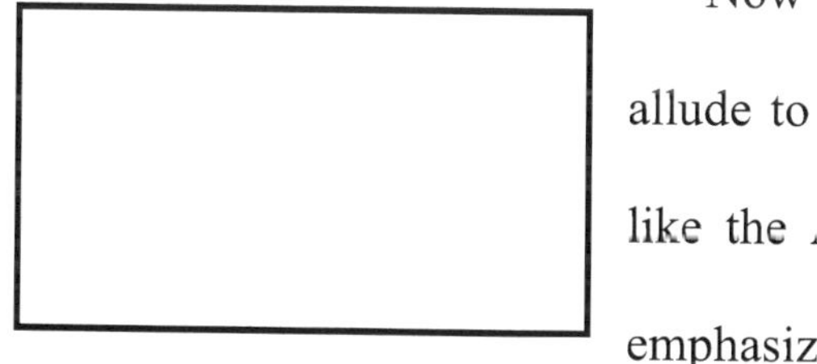

Now by no means do I allude to have gone through like the Apostle Paul. I am emphasizing the principle by which he put forth, that nothing he had gone through compared to the relationship he gained in Christ. As I look back over all I did encounter, nothing compares to what I have gained in Christ. All the achievements and accolades mean far less to me than the relationship I now enjoy with my Savior.

When I submitted to the will of God and the place of His planting, I heard Him speaking His purposes to me in a way I had never experienced before. As one example of many: I was given a vision to create an Empowerment Center that would address the need of the people in the community and those that transit the area. I had no idea how to do this in the natural, but God knew how to get it done. By FAITH in His ability, I moved forward to create the Empowerment Center He revealed to me.

I moved forward, not in my own strength or intellectual prowess--surely not, I was woefully inadequate--but in Christ, His super to my ability made me more than capable. I set forth with the attitude of Apostle Paul as He echoed these famous words:

"I can do all things through Christ which strengtheneth me." Philippians 4:13

"I have strength for all things in Christ who empowers me [I am ready for anything and equal to anything through Him who infuses inner strength into me; I am self sufficient in Christ's sufficiency]."Philippians 4:13 (The Amplified Bible)

I have learned through this experience, when you are planted where God wants you to be, you will be fruitful. Remember, when God gives a command to do something, everything we need to accomplish His purpose is in the command itself. I did my part to listen and obey. As I started doing the research, He provided me with the knowledge and understanding I needed. I wrote down the thoughts and concepts as God gave them to me and before I realized it, I had drafted a very detailed business plan to launch the Fisher Empowerment Center (FEC), Inc. Then God brought all the resources the FEC needed to launch. The FEC is founded upon a "One Stop" shop concept for community outreach services. Its goal is to foster individual and group empowerment by using a multiple pronged approach. God has used the FEC to truly bring empowerment to all those located in the community and all those residing in the neighboring counties. The word God used to stir my heart to undertake this task for outreach ministry is found in the gospel according to Luke:

> *"And the Lord said, Simon, Simon, behold, satan hath desired to have you, that he may sift you as wheat. But I have prayed for thee, that thy faith fail not: and when thou art converted (returned to me), strengthen thy brethren." Luke 22:31-32*

From the moment this word entered my spirit, I have been driven to strengthen my brothers and sisters in the Body of Christ. When our focus is on His focus, to strengthen others, every resource needed will be made manifest. I did not see the impact the FEC would have in the beginning, but I obeyed God. Now, the FEC is touching lives in every direction. Please visit us at www.gcecenter.org.

I am grateful that God gave me this opportunity to show forth His strength and wisdom. As a result of my obedience, God has brought me into contact with prominent men and women from around the globe. He wants to be seen in and through us; for His glory alone! However, this will not be reality until we are planted in the soil God purposed for us. The great King Solomon concluded this; fear God and keep His commandments.

In short, we were made to reproduce Him and His purpose here on earth. We are not called to reproduce anything of ourselves; no flesh will glory in the presence of God. We are to reproduce all that God is, and perpetuate His way by making deposits in the lives of others. When was the last time you made a deposit in the lives of those around you?

God will not change who He is, neither will He change the standard of living He has prescribed for us. When we meet His standard, everything that He is, we gain access to.

Take a moment and think about what I just said. You will have access to all that He is. With access to spiritual capital like that, how can we lose? I mentioned in Chapter 4, we cannot afford to lose. God wants our enemies to hear of the exploits He has wrought through His people. When they do, they will fear God and us.

> *"The people that know their God shall be strong and do exploits." Daniel 11:32*

I hear people say all the time, "You can't always win." My reply is, Why? I am the seed of Abraham in Christ, so my birthright coupled with my obedience gives me access to unlimited blessings, power and resources. The Lord said to Abraham (then Abram) in Genesis 12, the following:

> *I will make of thee a great nation*
> *I will bless thee*
> *I will make your name great*
> *You shall be a blessing*
> *I will bless them that bless thee*
> *I will curse him that curse thee*
> *In thee, all families in the earth are blessed.*

You tell me my brothers and sisters, where is it indicated in those promises a provision for losing? We inherited these promises by birthright, and they are activated by our obedience. Don't settle for less than what you are entitled to as being sons and daughters of God in Christ.

Cheese and Crackers

We grieve our Father when we settle for less that we should have. This reminds me of a story I heard a few years ago, and I often share it to reinforce what we have inherited in Christ.

A man lived in a foreign land and he had but one dream, to save enough money to get to the United States. The only way he could do that was to save enough money to purchase a ticket for one of the cruise ships that frequently visited his country. He worked hard and saved every penny he could to purchase a ticket.

Eventually he saved enough money, so he purchased a ticket for a trip to the United States. He said to himself, "I'd better save enough cheese and crackers to last me the entire trip." You see, in his mind he did not want to go hungry. Well, the day came, he boarded the vessel, and he was off. During the trip, each evening he would come up on deck where everyone was eating; but, he would not come in to sit down and eat himself. This continued the entire trip.

As the ship anchored outside New York City, waiting to enter port the next morning, the gentleman came up on deck and watched everyone eat. As he headed back down to his cabin for more cheese and crackers, a waiter stopped him. The waiter asked, "Sir, is there something wrong with the food?" The man answered, "No, not at all. It looks and smells so good!" The waiter said, "Sir, I am confused. You say it looks and smells good, yet, each evening, I have watched you standing outside, looking in at everyone else eating, and never coming in to eat yourself." The man replied, "I did not have any extra money to buy food. The waiter said, "Dear sir, didn't you know that when you purchased the ticket all the food was included?" My brothers and sisters, dear friends, this man settled for eating cheese and crackers, even though he had access to much more.

So many settle for far less, even though they have access to all that God is. Are you going to settle for cheese and crackers when you can eat the best there is? That's what we are doing beloved if we are losing and going without. God has made provision in Christ for believers to live a victorious life, a life of abundance, with no lack. Do you believe His word? Then if you do, stop settling! Remove the reproach of the enemy off your life. You are the seed of Abraham! Ought not you, too, be loosed from your infirmity?

ENDNOTES/SCRIPTURES

1. I Samuel 1
2. II Timothy 3:5
3. Daniel 11:32
4. Genesis 12:2

WILL YOU BE ISAAC?

"And he said, behold the fire and the wood: but where is the lamb for a burnt offering?"
Genesis 22:7

In this chapter there are two major characters, Abraham (father of a multitude), originally Abram (high father), who was the first great patriarch of the Book of Genesis and Isaac (laughter), the son of promise. They each have a tremendous story to tell based upon their relationship with God the Father and to each other. Let me briefly highlight some of the things that have transpired in the life of

Abraham that will set the stage for our theme in Genesis, Chapter 22, "Will you be Isaac?"

In Genesis, Chapter 15, Abram wanted to know what the Lord would give him, so he makes a pitch for Eliezer, his servant, that he might be his heir. God rejected this idea. He told Abram that he would bring forth an heir from his own bowels. God makes it known that this heir will be a product of Abram and Sarai and through them He will give birth to a nation. He makes a covenant with Abram and promises that He has given his seed the land. Shortly

thereafter, Sarai gets the idea that it would be good if Abram would go in to her hand maiden, Hagar, so that she could have children through her. Abram, like us, for a brief moment, forgot what the Lord spoke to him and yielded to the advice that sounded good and appeared to be in alignment with what God wanted for him. As a result of Sarai's head (human reasoning), and Abram's loins (human strength), Ishmael is born. Needless to say, this did not please God. Understand this; God does not need man's wisdom and strength to fulfill His purpose. I am reminded of an article I read some time ago. The article read, "If you ever want to make God laugh, tell Him your plan for your life." In fact, the apostle James saw this approach as being arrogant; to think we can accomplish His purpose in human strength. He stated:

> *"For that ye ought to say, If the Lord will, we shall live, and do this, or that." James 4:15*

All God has ever needed is a person to listen to Him, and when He has that person, He can do great exploits.

Disobedience Renders One Dull Of Hearing

Now consider this as it pertains to the birth of Ishmael. Abraham was 86 years old when Ishmael was born, and sad to say, God did not speak to him again until he was 99.

That's 13 years! 13 denotes rebellion and judgment. You see my friend, at 86, Abram was still strong enough physically to produce a child. I can imagine God said, *"I will wait you out Abram. I will wait until you can no longer produce on your own, therefore, you will no longer be able to interfere with my plan."* In other words, He waited until Abram and Sarai's bodies were dead with regards to reproduction.

Make no mistake; God will wait us out as well. He will wait until you and I can no longer rely upon our own wisdom and strength. Our strength may be in money, fame, success, etc. Whatever our dependence, if it is not upon the Lord and His word, He will wait until it can no longer be used to interfere with His plan for us. Think about it. Abram's actions triggered thirteen years of silence from God. Can you imagine being cut off like that? How many of us at one point in our lives were accustomed to hearing the voice of the Lord, but out of disobedience, His voice could no longer be heard? What a miserable feeling. We longed for His voice like never before. Why? Because we finally realize just how precious communication with Him is. It was only when we were truly repentant and sought Him with our whole heart did He speak to us, thus, reconnecting us into fellowship. Do you remember how excited you were to have restored that which was lost? You can imagine then how excited Abram felt to once again hear the Lord's voice.

Communication Restored

Genesis 17 records the dialogue God begins again with His servant. He appears to Abram and identifies Himself as the Almighty God, or El Shaddai, which means "God, all sufficient, the breasted one, the nourisher, the sustainer." This reveals God as both Father and Mother. He then commands Abram to walk before Him and be perfect (upright, sincere). He renews His covenant, and changes Abram's name to Abraham, and Sarai (dominative; a head person) to Sarah (mistress, female noble). Remember my dear friend, when God changes a name, it represents a change in one's nature. Keep in mind, God has not changed His mind about Abraham and Sarah bringing forth an heir. God speaks to Abraham saying:

> *"Sarah thy wife shall bear thee a son indeed; and thou shalt call his name Isaac: and I will establish my covenant with him for an everlasting covenant and with his seed after him." Genesis 17:19*

Are you glad that God does not give up on us when we make mistakes along the way? He is determined to bring about His purpose in us and I am grateful He is longsuffering with us. All that He spoke to Abraham, He has brought to fulfillment:

> *"And the Lord visited Sarah as he had said, and the Lord did unto Sarah as he had spoken. For Sarah conceived, and bare Abraham a son in his old age, at the set time of which God had spoken to him. And Abraham called the name of his son that was born unto him, whom Sarah bare to him, Isaac."*
> *Genesis 21:1-3*

He Is Faithful That Promised

I want to bring your attention to these powerful words, "And the Lord did unto Sarah as He had spoken!" The Lord our God cannot lie, and every word that He speaks is a guarantee. He secures the word He speaks by His own name. In other words, since there is no other greater than Himself, He has put Himself under oath to do all that He utters. Hallelujah to His name! God has proven to Abraham He can be trusted, for He has through His sovereignty and providence, brought forth the son of promise through vessels that were dead in the natural, but made capable of the purpose of God by the word of His power!

Consider this fact! Whatever word God has spoken over your life has not returned to God. He made a promise to each of us that His word would not return to Him void (Isaiah 55:11). That means, it will not return until it has brought fulfillment. Look behind you. That word is still following you in the earth realm and it will do so until you position yourself before God. When you do, the word will do what it was sent to do. Then, and only then, will it return to God.

Returning the Gift to God

As we continue our journey with Abraham, we see that he has touched and handled the son of promise: Isaac, whose name means laughter, or God smiles. A relationship between them has been built and it is founded upon the principles of God. Over time, Isaac has watched his father, Abraham, in his obedience to the things of the Lord his God. This same obedience is being sown in Isaac. He is aware of the God of Abraham and how to worship Him. As we look through the telescope of time back into Genesis 22, we see that God approaches Abraham and gives a very lofty command,

GIVE ME ISAAC! He is to offer Isaac as a sacrifice to the God he loves. Are you willing to give to God your Isaac? Isaac can be that one person, place or thing you love above all else. Can you hear Him saying to you now, GIVE ME YOUR ISAAC? Sure you can! Yield to the love call of God. Bring Him your Isaac, bound and ready to be offered. Then God can say, "I know that you will not withhold anything from me."

> *"And it came to pass after these things, that God did tempt Abraham, and said unto him, Abraham, and he said, behold, here I am. And he said, take now thy son, thine only son Isaac, whom thou lovest, and get thee into the land of Moriah; and offer him there for a burnt offering upon one of the mountains which I will tell thee of." Genesis 22:1-2*

Can you imagine it? Abraham and Sarah waited long for their consolation from the Lord and now God wants him back. You can understand why Abraham is called the father of faith. Without hesitation, Abraham gathered up all he needed for his journey to Mount Moriah. He staggered not at the promises of God. His obedience serves as a beacon of light to this day for all of us. Nothing should be that precious to us that we cannot part ways with it, for His sake. As Abraham, Isaac, and the men make their ascent up the mountain, they approached the place God had told him of. Then Abraham stopped a moment to prophesy to the young men. He said, you guys stay right here, while the lad and I go up the mountain to worship, and we will come again unto you. Did you hear the prophetic word? Abraham said, *"We will come again unto you."* I believe Abraham was saying this, I will go and offer Isaac, but before we come back down the mountain, God will raise him from the dead, based upon the promise that the covenant with Isaac is an everlasting covenant. Isaac cannot exercise the covenant if he is dead.

What a powerful picture! No matter what happens in our lives, if God has promised something, stand on it! Abraham was convinced that no matter what happened up on Mount Moriah, Isaac was coming back with him. As they continued upward, Isaac realized that an important piece of the worship service was missing. He says to his father, "I see the fire and the wood: but where is the LAMB for a burnt offering?" The spirit of prophecy moved heavily upon Abraham, for he would prophesy yet again.

> *"And Abraham said, my son, God will provide himself a lamb for a burnt offering: so they went both of them together." Genesis 22:8*

Wow! What a profound declaration. Notice, he did not say God would provide a lamb to sacrifice, he said, God would provide HIMSELF a lamb. In way of typology, Abraham spoke of God becoming flesh, and offering Himself as the sacrifice, or the Lamb that would be slain for the entire world. Praise Him! Abraham in a sense was advertising the fact that since he was offering up his son, God would give His son   (Jesus) as well. Simply put, God would wrap Himself in flesh, and serve as the ultimate sacrifice. This prophecy has been fulfilled.

"And the Word was made flesh, and dwelt among us. And we beheld his glory, the glory as the only begotten of the Father, full of grace and truth."
John 1:14

Now, let's continue our ascent with Abraham and Isaac. As they arrived to the place, Abraham did not delay; he was not having second thoughts about obeying God. He immediately erected an altar, laid the wood in place, and then bound Isaac and laid him upon it. He took the knife and raised it to slay Isaac. When Abraham did this, God called to him and told him to stay his hand. He was not to harm Isaac. You see beloved, in God's eyes, Isaac died. Here we see again the type of Christ that died and resurrected on the Third day. Consider Abraham and Isaac's actions, as well as God's response:

"And they came to the place which God had told him of; and Abraham built an altar there, and laid the wood in order, and bound Isaac his son, and laid him on the altar upon the wood. And Abraham stretched forth his hand, and took the knife to slay

his son And the angel of the Lord called unto him out of heaven, and said, Abraham, Abraham: and he said, here I am. And he said, lay not thine hand upon the lad, neither do thou anything unto him: for now I know that thou fearest God, seeing thou hast not withheld thy son, thine only son from me."
Genesis 22:9-12

No matter how much he loved Isaac, Abraham was committed to being in sync with God's will. Whatever your situation might be, link your confession and actions to the promises of God. When we synchronize our walk and talk with heaven's will, we, too, will receive a word from heaven, affirming the same.

As Abraham did not mind bruising Isaac for the Lord's sake, Isaiah 53:10 reveals that God returned the favor, *"Yet it pleased the Lord to bruise him; he hath put him to grief."* Thank God for the obedience of Abraham! Because of it, God was now obligated to do the same.

Total Submission to the Father's Will

Now let's shift our focus on Isaac's actions for a moment. Isaac served as a type of Christ. Remember, I asked on the outset, would you be an Isaac? Consider how Isaac, being a young lad, not a little boy, never resisted. He did not fight nor struggle with the will of his own Father. He let Abraham bind him and lay him on the Altar. He, like Jesus, was as a lamb led to its shearers; he was dumb and did not open his mouth. He completely surrendered his life into the hands of his father, whom he believed in, without reservation. Will we come like Isaac? Will we allow our Father to bind us and lay us upon the altar so we might die and be resurrected in Him? The Apostle Paul declared this truth to the church in Galatia:

> *"I have been crucified with Christ, nevertheless I live, yet not I, but Christ liveth in me, and the life which I now live in the flesh, I live by the faith of the son of God, who loved me and gave himself for me." Galatians 2:20*

Isaac, as did our Lord Jesus, fell into the ground and died, and brought forth much fruit.

Will you? As we look at Isaac, keep in mind what Jesus spoke according to John:

"Verily, Verily, I say unto you, except a corn of wheat fall into the ground and die, it abideth alone, but if it die, it brings forth much fruit." John 12:24

I want to focus for a moment on the word "fall." It presupposes a yielding; there is no fight, no struggle. Bear this in mind as it pertains to Isaac, a type of Christ, and the life of the believer. Have we yielded to the will of the Father or are we still fighting and struggling with Him? If we yield, we die to ourselves, our way of being, and how we do things. We then give way to be planted in the soil that God has chosen for us. The soil (environment) He has chosen prepares us to be cracked and reshaped for the production of fruit. Many don't want to go through this process so they resist the hand of the Father. When they resist, they hinder the plan of God and their ability to bring forth fruit to His glory.

All the while Abraham is proving His obedience to God

in the offering of Isaac, God has kept the ram concealed from him. Think about it for a moment. Abraham never saw, neither did he hear the ram that was caught in the thicket right behind him.

> *"And Abraham lifted up his eyes, and looked, and behold behind him a ram caught in a thicket by his horns: and Abraham went and took the ram, and offered him up for a burnt offering in the stead of his son." And Abraham called the name of that place Jehovah-Jireh: as it is said to this day. In the mount of the Lord it shall be seen." Genesis 22:13-14*

Beloved, just as Abraham never saw, neither heard the ram until he fully complied with the will of God, so it is with us. God has already sent the provision ahead of us; we will not see it until we have complied with His will. Then we will say like Abraham, this place is Jehovah-Jireh. The scripture declares that Abraham removed Isaac from the Altar, and put the ram that God had provided upon it. He sacrificed unto God and started his descent down the mountain. The young men see Abraham and Isaac are coming down the mountain; however, they are totally unaware of what just transpired. Abraham and Isaac knew of their ordeal, but they are overjoyed that they have met God's requirement of true love and commitment. Their faith is reinforced and their vision of God enlarged. Nowhere in scripture does it say they told the young men or Sarah what happened. Some of our encounters with God are not to be spoken of to others, because it was just for us and our growth. Like John on the Isle of Patmos, we are sometimes told to close the book. Become that Isaac today, end the struggle, fall into the ground, die to your way and experience a true resurrection, as did our heavenly Isaac.

As believers, we can learn so much from how Abraham and Isaac lived, worshipped, and most importantly, how they responded to the will of the Father.

ENDNOTES

1. Genesis 22:7
2. Genesis 15
3. James 4:15
4. Genesis 17:19

5. Genesis 21:1-3
6. Isaiah 55:11
7. Genesis 22:1-2
8. Genesis 22:8
9. John 1:14
10. Genesis 22:9-14
11. Isaiah 53:10
12. Galatians 2:20
13. John 12:24

THE LION AND THE BEAR

"And David said, thy servant slew the Lion and the Bear, this Philistine shall be as one of them." I Samuel 17:36

In every facet of life, from infancy to adulthood, God has been the initiator of relationship. I find it necessary to keep repeating this because I don't ever want you to forget the fact that God started the relationship we now enjoy and He will surely finish it. By the mere fact that we have knowledge of Him starting us out on this journey, we understand that this puts Him right in the center of our lives, and therefore, responsible for bringing us to the place

He has envisioned. Like a composer of a symphony, He is orchestrating events and situations that are necessary for our growth and success and will ultimately shape us until we look just like Jesus. That does not mean we like going through everything, but we trust God that it all will work for our good. Keep in mind that as we go through the various challenges in life, they paint a vivid picture of our love and obedience toward God, our ability to be used of Him and how we represent His name. We would call this an impressive resume. That is exactly what God has been doing in you and me my friend. He has been building a resume so that others will know what you are qualified to do in Him. Be comforted therefore in knowing that nothing just happens in this life without a purpose.

God is a Resume Builder

As we know, David was a type of Christ. We can draw from the things he did in life and compare them to the things Jesus did on our behalf. In particular, I find it fascinating how God used David to free an army from the tyranny of one man, Goliath. This one man paralyzed the army of Israel, as did satan paralyze humanity in the crucible of sin. Israel needed a champion to go out and fight this renowned warrior. Likewise, we needed a champion that would go before us to free us from the bondage and corruption of sin. Hail to our champion, the Lord Jesus Christ! In his day, David became qualified to bring about the demise of the tyrant of the day.

> *"Now the Philistines gathered together their armies to battle, and were gathered together at Shochoh, which belongeth to Judah, and pitched between Shochoh and Azekah, in Ephes-dammim. And Saul and the men of Israel were gathered together and pitched by the valley of Elah, and set the battle in array against the Philistines." I Samuel 17:1-2*

The battle lines have been drawn; the army of Israel is paralyzed. In their confidence, the Philistines have made a critical and tactical error. They are caught between Judah (Praise), and Ephes-dammim (Field of Blood). It is a terrible thing to be caught between praise and the blood. Wow! What enemy can stand? Bible history records that Goliath had been coming out and challenging the host of

Israel for 40 days. (Note: The number 40 represents probation. His time for destruction had come.) And while

Israel's champion is not yet on the scene, he is on the way. The God of Israel has been preparing him for such a time as this one. Do not fret my brothers and sisters; you, too, are being prepared for an occasion not yet seen. Let God the Father have His way with you. Someone needs to be free and God is sending you to bring that freedom. Get ready!

God's Public Debut of David

Jesse calls David out of the field to take food to his brothers and cheeses for their captain. He is to look in on his brothers to see how they are doing. I love how God uses people in our circle to get us where we need to be. God needed David on the scene of the battle, so He moves on Jesse to think about his sons in the war. David obeys his father and goes to check on his brothers. Even though Israel does not know it, their champion has arrived. Make no mistake about it, when God's chosen is on the scene, change is coming!

> *"And as he (David) talked with them (his brothers), behold, there came up the champion, the Philistine of Gath, Goliath by name, out of the armies of the Philistines, and spake according to the same words: and David heard them." I Samuel 17:23*

Take careful notice that Goliath did not speak anything different than he had spoken for the past 40 days. The only difference is that David heard his words. Upon hearing his words, David became infuriated. David understood that these words from the enemy brought reproach upon Israel and defiance against the living God.

> *"And David spake to the men that stood by him, saying, What shall be done to the man that killeth this Philistine, and taketh away the reproach from Israel? For who is this uncircumcised Philistine, that he should defy the armies of the living God?" I Samuel 17:26*

David took a stand for righteousness and honor of the name of the Lord. When David's brothers heard him speak to the men, they were not at all happy. They were more focused on whom he left the sheep with, than the reproach the enemy put on them. When you take a stand to do right before God and man, many will accuse you of having ulterior motives. They accused David of being naughty. I like David's response:

> *"And David said, What have I now done? Is there not a cause?" I Samuel 17:29*

David put his brothers on the spot by asking them, "Is there not a cause?" Beware my brothers and sisters; once you start taking a stand, people around you will become offended and threatened by you. The reason for this is because in their hearts, they know they should have already been addressing the problem. They will not like the fact that you had to come on the scene to do what they should have been doing. When this opposition comes, stand your ground like David did. When you do, your words and actions will have an impact on those around you and they will come before great men and women. These individuals will be able to propel you into the position that God has ordained. David's words were rehearsed before the king, and when the king heard them, he called for David to be brought forth. David moved from the field to the king's tent. Why? Because in his private life; David had allowed God to prepare him for this moment.

David's Resume

In I Samuel 17, King Saul told David he was not able to go out to fight with Goliath, a man of war from his youth. However, David's response is resounding, even unto this day. He explained that when he kept his father's sheep, a lion and a bear came and took a sheep out of the fold, and when they rose against him, he smote them. He slew both the Lion and the Bear and now Goliath is about to become as both of them.

Beloved, David was successful primarily because he defeated the Lion and the Bear. If you have not dealt with the Lion and the Bear in your private arena, I can assure you, you will not have the opportunity to face Goliath in the public arena. Facing Goliath is a privilege. It is granted once we conquer the Lion and the Bear in PRIVATE. David conquered in private, so must we!

Many believers are outstanding during the service on Sunday and other days of gathering. Yet these same individuals go home where the Lion and the Bear dominate them. This must change! Moab was judged because he did not change. His scent remained the same. The Bible says he was not poured out from vessel to vessel. Jeremiah illustrates this principle:

> *"If the footmen weary thee, how can you contend with horses? And if in the time of peace you get weary, how will you handle the swelling of the Jordan?" Jeremiah 12:5*

What does all this mean? As there is a natural progression in life, there is also a spiritual progression. Ignoring this principle will invite great peril in the life of the believer. As we encounter each level of this walk with God, we must remember, our dependence is, and always shall be, upon God. David's confidence in slaying Goliath was in these words, "The same God that delivered me from the Lion and the Bear shall deliver this Philistine into my hands."

Walking in the Light of Christ

Cockroach Christians: You may not be able to identify with this topic if you have never encountered a cockroach. Growing up, I used to always get up at night to either use the bathroom or attempt to sneak in the kitchen to have my way with Mom's leftovers. Well, I recall turning on the lights and noticed what appeared to be hundreds of cockroaches scattering in every direction. Their worst enemy had come suddenly upon them. Who, or better yet, what, was there enemy? You guessed it, the light! The cockroaches scattered because the light exposed them. Their preferred environment is darkness. Take heed that we do not display this characteristic. That is, when light shows up, we scatter like the cockroaches. The Bible tells us that when light comes, walk in the light.

To come to the light as the scripture suggests means that a person is ready to expose every part of their lives to the light. In short, this person is saying, "I am ready to conquer in private, no more being a hypocrite or having a form of godliness, but in private denying the power thereof." Let me warn you dear reader, this is a very painful, albeit, necessary, step in the process of victory. You see, any matter that is concealed is in darkness, and it is in this darkness, the concealed matter thrives and perpetuates. So, when a decision is made to walk in the light, satan loses his grip on you. Praise God! Think about the alternative; if we decide to cover issues in our lives under the shroud of darkness, the peace and security that is promised us is forfeited. Fear, anxiety, paranoia and ultimately defeat consumes us. God cannot put you and me on display publicly if we have not mastered the lower level of our preparation for being kings and priests.

If I may, let me take you back to David when he faced the Lion and the Bear. As David was in the field watching the Father's sheep, he was being trained, not just as a natural shepherd, but also as king. The Bible tells us that we are kings and priests unto our God, but as long as we are babes, we cannot be released in this dimension of authority and power. We need to be under trainers. Let me reiterate, God wants to put you and I on display so the world can see Him!

How disappointing it must be to the Father? Knowing He has made provision for us to live a victorious life; yet, we choose to lose. There was a prophetic word conveyed to us in song years ago saying, "What's wrong with my children, and why won't they praise me? I've given them everything, still they have no

joy." There is no joy because His people refuse to walk in the light.

Once we have confessed the Lord Jesus, we cannot keep sin concealed in our lives. We must allow Him to shine His light on every area concerning us. When we live our lives trying to keep certain things (sin) under wraps, we  are a people most miserable. I don't care who you are, if you have tasted of the goodness of His grace and have certain aspects of your life concealed, YOU are most miserable. God speaks light and life to these areas because He knows we will not experience the benefits of His finished work as long as they are hidden from the light.

Beloved, I tried at one point to live my life in the public arena, yet concealing issues in my private arena. The Lord of all mercy ministered to me and it was an awakening moment. He allowed me to see the results of the decisions I had made and was about to make. His light shined in my heart and I saw the devastation of my actions should I had continued down that path. In an instant, I saw the lives, young and old, that would have been impacted by my decision to continue to conceal sin. As the light of Christ made my heart free, I knew my life would never be the same; neither would those in my circle. You see beloved, for the first time, I did not see exposing my issue to the light as loss; rather, it was gain from the truest sense. I chose to run into the light, and as a result, became truly free. I conquered the lion and the bear in private; satan could no longer hold me, nor is he able to hold you if you so choose to come to the light. Will you choose to conquer your Lion so you can advance to the Bear, or will you remain on level one?

There is so much more that awaits those progressing in kingdom principles. Cast off fear; it cannot survive in light. Is not this an amazing revelation of just how God, through the person of Jesus Christ, has rendered our adversary powerless against us? And when we make choices to come to the light, despite all the credit the church gives him, our adversary could not stop us from coming. Seed of Abraham, rise up and take your place! No longer are you to wait for the crumbs that fall from the master's table. Come to the light and sit down at the table and see where all the crumbs are coming from. I make this declaration over your life, in the name of Jesus Christ:

> *"You shall decree a thing, and it shall be established unto you, and the light shall shine upon your path."* Job 22:28

Now, right now, to you, I so decree, that is, I prophesy, faith toward God and His word and victory over your life. No longer will you walk in fear and no longer will you be afraid of light. You will welcome light into the smallest crevices of your life, and as you do, darkness will flee and you will take your place on the hill with the saints in light. In Jesus' Name, it is so!

ENDNOTES

1. I Samuel 17
2. Jeremiah 12:5
3. Job 22:28

WHAT THE PRODIGAL SON TELLS US

"And took his journey into a far country, and there wasted his substance with riotous living." Luke 15:13

There are times in our lives when we miss the mark and even lose our way. God does not abandon us when we do so; on the contrary, He immediately pursues the course of action that will bring us home. Just ask Jonah. He greatly errored in the faith, and as a result, put others at risk. God set out to get Jonah. He had purpose for him and his act of disobedience did not change God's mind. He created the right situation, or storm, for Jonah. The storm was to help Jonah realize the error of his ways. Here again, God is determined to cultivate the relationship He has started with Jonah. His love covered Jonah's sin. Jonah could not outrun the plan and purpose God had for him. Jonah had become a prodigal son; however, because of the grace of God, he would not remain one. This leads me to our next topic; the prodigal son.

Before Being Prodigal

To be prodigal means to be wasteful, reckless, ncontrolled and extravagant. Well, there was a time in the younger son's life when he was never wasteful, reckless, 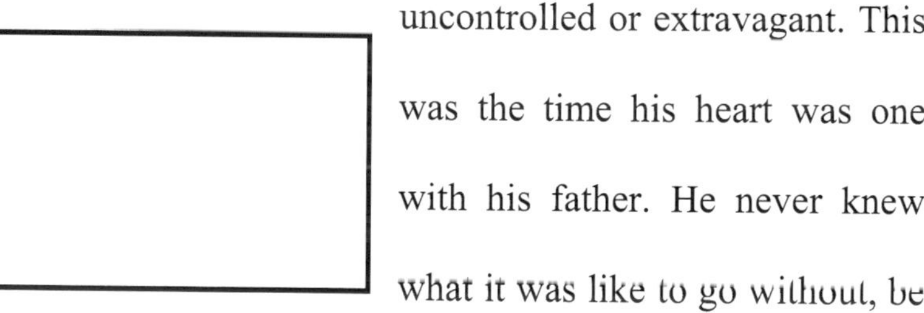 uncontrolled or extravagant. This was the time his heart was one with his father. He never knew what it was like to go without, be destitute, lonely, and without direction. Along the way, as the younger son was serving the father, he gave place to the devil. As a result, the enemy planted a bad seed in his mind. The seed he planted was this; he convinced the younger son that he could do better outside the father's house. So before he ever confronted his father for his inheritance, his heart was already in some distant land. In our day, we have so many that are physically in the father's house, but their hearts are in some distant land. Jesus, being well aware of this condition in His people stated:

> *"This people draweth nigh unto me with their mouth, and honoureth me with their lips; but their heart is far from me." Matthew 15:8*

The younger son dreamed of enjoying his freedom far away from his father and older brother. He wanted to have his own way, and that selfishness moved him to leave his father's house, thus, leaving his father with a broken heart. Does this sound familiar? We want our freedom to live as we wish; so much so, we leave the comforts and protection of our heavenly Father's house, thus, breaking His heart. Only when we abide in the Father's house can we expect to experience of His bounty.

"Abide in me, and I in you. As the branch cannot bear fruit of itself, except it abide in the vine; no more can ye, except ye abide in me. If ye abide in me, and my words abide in you, ye shall ask what ye will, and it shall be done unto you." John 15:4,7
"Live in me. Make your home in me just as I do in you. In the same way that a branch can't bear grapes by itself but only by being joined to the vine, you can't bear fruit unless you are joined with me. But if you make yourselves at home with me and my words are at home in you, you can be sure that whatever you ask will be listened to and acted upon." John 15:4,7 (The Message Bible)

When we, in our hearts, are not with the Father, it is not a surprise, then, when we do not experience all that the Father is. Do we think that He does not know who is with Him? He knows the thoughts and the intents of our hearts. How would you feel to be surrounded by your children, yet all the while knowing they did not want to be with you? In their hearts, there is a call, beckoning them to come to some other place, far away from you. We would feel terrible! And like the father of the younger son, we, too, would be watching the road everyday, hoping that our child makes it back home. You see my brothers and sisters, the father knew the hardships his son would face without him.

His hope was that someday his son would come to his senses, and in that awareness, come home. There was so much the younger son had to learn in life, and because of his decisions, he would indeed learn just how much he needed his father. Until now, he never experienced lack, neither did he know what life was like not to have the father there to guide him. These things are certainly the beginning of sorrow.

Casting Off Restraint

The younger son illustrated what we will all do when we lose our vision. There remains nothing to encourage us to keep on track, and as a result, we exercise no self-control:

"My people are destroyed for lack of knowledge."
Hosea 4:6

When he cast off restraint, he was no longer content with living in the father's house. This reminds me of what

Thomas Huxley[4] said, "A man's worst difficulties begin when he is able to do just as he likes." When we find ourselves living with no restraints, we begin to pierce ourselves through with many sorrows. And as we see, with no vision, the plight of the younger son begins:

> *"And he said, a certain man had two sons. And the younger of them said to his father, Father, give me the portion of goods that falleth. And he divided unto them his living. And not many days after the younger son gathered all together, and took his journey into a far country, and there wasted his substance with riotous living." Luke 15:11-13*

The younger son has followed the leading of the supplanter (satan) by leaving his father's house. He is about to learn the hard way that we will have a difficult time enjoying the things money can buy, when we have not learned the things money cannot buy. You see my beloved, we need to be resolved that there are some things about us that will never

---

[4] Huxley was an English Biologist, an advocate of the Darwin Theory

be for sale. The enemy has the younger son exactly where he wants him, away from the father. Away from the father, the younger son has become a weak link in the chain; prey for the enemy. Yet, in the son's mind, all is well. Does this sound familiar? He lulled the younger son into thinking that he made the right decision by leaving home. Think about it. He is living larger than he ever has and he is surrounded by many friends who project love for him; all the while, they are agents of satan. This is what the enemy wants from us, to lull us to sleep and try to convince us that outside the Father's house is so much better for us. He whispers in our ears, telling us that we can live free from all the rules the Father has placed on us. Have you ever noticed when believers are outside the will of God, how much more popular they become? Don't believe all the hype. When we are practicing sin and popularity grows, a red flag should go up, and an alarm should be sounding in our spirit. It is all a smoke screen to keep you and me from ever realizing just how much trouble we might be in. By the time we realize it, we have lost so much, and more often than not, hurt so many people along the way.

> *"There is a way which seemeth right unto a man, but the end thereof are the ways of death."*
> *Proverbs 14:12*

Sin always promises freedom and pleasure, but brings about slavery and death. While the younger son was away, the father never lost hope. He remained ever vigilant in his watch for him, no doubt wondering how much his son has suffered. I imagine he thought often, and even said to himself, maybe this is the day my son will return home.

While Being Prodigal

At this point, the son has truly become prodigal (wasteful, reckless, uncontrolled, and extravagant).

> *"And when he had spent all, there arose a mighty famine in that land; and he began to be in want. And he went and joined himself to a citizen of that country; and he sent him into his fields to feed swine." Luke 15:14-15*

Remember, the prodigal son was living large, instant popularity was his, and he was surrounded by many friends. The prodigal son was lulled to sleep by satan's lullaby; he was oblivious to the withdrawals his circle of friends were making. They did not do anything to strengthen him or make him better off. They just kept sucking the life and resources from him. Let this be a critical lesson for us as believers. Beware of those who always make   withdrawals from you, yet never make any deposits.

"Iron sharpeneth iron, so shall a man sharpeneth the countenance of his friend." *Proverbs 27:17*

How many people are in your circle? How often have they made deposits in your life that enhance you and your relationship with the Lord? This is an important step in Christian maturity; knowing those within our circle and what they bring to us.

Nature Determines Association

Let me use the analogy of eagles and buzzards for a moment to illustrate how we should choose associates. If you want to be and fly like an eagle, then you need to associate yourself with other eagles. Only an eagle can show another how to become an eagle. Remember, nature determines association. A buzzard will migrate to the company of other buzzards. Why? Because they have the same character and nature; they like eating those things which are dead. If you want something with life in it, find another eagle. The scriptures have often related the people of God to an eagle and its attributes. Of particular note is its vigilance even while molting, or transforming. Of all the birds of prey, it is said that the eagle is the only one that never loses its ability of flight. When other birds of prey are molting, they become prey to the enemy. The eagle is always ready to take flight.

Consider how both the eagle and buzzard mentality is displayed when one undergoes trials. When a believer has a buzzard mentality, it is evident by what they say during the trial. Their conversation during the time of trial is filled with doubt and defeat; a meal fit for a buzzard. The eagle, well, it will steer clear of a meal like this one. It will look for something with more life in it. When you go through trials, find that one person that will speak life into your heart, to keep you vigilant and always ready to take flight.

The enemy would like nothing better than to see your life drained from you, leaving you helpless and destitute. This will happen when we leave the Father in heaven and try guiding ourselves. There are spiritual landmines the enemy has laid for us, and without the Lord going before us we will surely become casualties of war.

The Awakening

As we previously mentioned, the prodigal son has lost all his money; and as a result, his popularity took flight. Now, his condition is dire, yet, help outside the father cannot be found. He is reduced to feeding swine. This father's son is now living well beneath what his birthright afforded him.

> *"And he would have fain have filled his belly with the husks that the swine did eat; and no man gave unto him. And when he came to himself, he said, how many hired servants of my father's have bread enough and to spare, and I perish with hunger! I will arise and go to my father, and I will say unto him, Father, I have sinned against heaven, and before thee, and am no more worthy to be called thy son: make me as one of thy hired servants."*
> *Luke 15:16-19*

All the painful circumstances that have befallen the prodigal son served as invaluable tools to help shape his character and attitude. He now remembers the goodness of his father and how he takes care of even the servants of his house. I can only imagine that he said to himself, if my father is this good to servants, perhaps he will be willing to forgive his son? The word declares:

> *"The Lord hath appeared of old unto me, saying, yea, I have loved thee with an everlasting love: therefore with lovingkindness have I drawn thee."*
> *Jeremiah 31:3*

The memory of his father's goodness brought him to repentance. People we love and care about may be in the pigpen today, but as long as they are still alive, there is hope that they, too, will come to themselves and come home. Well, let's see what reaction the prodigal son received as he returned home.

Return of the Son

The son is on his way home, rehearsing what he will say to his father. The reason he is rehearsing is because he does not know the depth of his father's love for him. He is like so many today; they hesitate coming back to their heavenly Father because they have been convinced that He couldn't possibly forgive them.

> *"And he arose, and came to his father, but when he was yet a great way off, his father saw him, and had compassion, and ran, and fell on his neck, and kissed him." Luke 15:20*

I want you to remember the father was vigilant in his watching for his son to return home. He had an expectation, therefore he watched for him. A point of emphasis must be put on the fact that the father ran toward his son. Men of the East did not run; it was undignified to do so. Yet, this man ran to him. Perhaps it was because the father did not know how the community would treat his son. Especially since everyone knew that his son asked for his inheritance and left home. It was a sign of disrespect for children to ask for their inheritance early, that is, before their parents' death. His action could have been misunderstood and taken that the younger son was saying that I wish you would die already. According to the Law of Moses, a son that brought dishonor to his father was to be stoned to death. If he was mindful of this, he may have been trying to protect his son from this requirement, and therefore willing to be hit himself. This is a powerful picture of the redemption story. God so loved the world that He put Himself, in the person of Jesus, in judgment's path. He tasted death for every man

"But we see Jesus, who was made a little lower than the angels for the suffering of death, crowned with glory and honour; that He by the grace of God should taste death for every man." Hebrews 2:9

The father ran to his son and kissed him. His son confessed all that he rehearsed to the father. The father was so elated that his son was alive and that he returned home that he gave instructions to celebrate with a feast. His father never once said, I told you so, or pulled out a ledger revealing how much he gave to his son, or how many mistakes he made. He simply received him back into his presence. The prodigal son experienced a restoration to his rightful place. We, too, have a heavenly Father, waiting with expectation, that one day, His sons and daughters will return home and take their rightful place.

ENDNOTES/SCRIPTURES

1. Matthew 15:8
2. John 15:4,7
3. The Message Bible
4. Hosea 4:6
5. Luke 15:11-13
6. Proverbs 14:12
7. Luke 15:14-15
8. Proverbs 27:17
9. Luke 15:16-19
10. Jeremiah 31:3
11. Luke 15:20
12. Hebrews 2:9

10

LOVE MADE PERFECT

"Herein is our love made perfect."
I John 4:17

As we respond more and more to God's pursuit of us, we learn to love more like Him. This is vitally important, especially as it pertains to those who have rejected the message of Christ, and those who have turned back into the world after having knowledge of Christ. I have seen the liberating and transforming power of God's love first hand. My brothers and sisters, I was one who had drifted off the path of the Lord at one point in my life. I had repented for my errors and was even restored into fellowship with the

Lord. However, there was still a need in my heart to truly be received among those that I held in high regard in the faith. My beloved, we can never underestimate the power of a hug, warm smile, or a kind word. You never know those around you who are in need of a touch of God's Love.

Before I go any further about my restoration among the brothers and sisters, let me share with you a story I read some time ago that illustrates the liberating and transforming power of love and kindness. A young boy was walking home from school one day with all his books in his hand. He decided to clear out his locker. On his way home, bullies came by and knocked the books out of his hand. There was another young man nearby that witnessed what had happened. He walked over to him and helped him carry his books. As they walked and talked with each other, they discovered that they lived close to each other, and as a result of a small gesture of kindness, they became really good friends. Well, time passed and it was graduating day for two young men who became close friends. During the high school graduation ceremony, the young man I   mentioned that had the arm full of books served as the   Valedictorian. During his speech he said something that shocked everyone. He said, "One day I had cleaned my locker out and was carrying my books home with plans to kill myself." At this point you could hear a pin drop. This young man had become one of the most popular students in school. He said if it was not for the kindness a young man, (now his best friend) showed to him that day; he would have surely killed himself. This young man made a different choice because of the love and kindness of one person. We all must be ready to demonstrate the love God has deposited in us. We never know who might be thinking about taking their lives or just doing something harmful and destructive to others. It could be people in your circle, people you see every day. The word declares:

"Herein is our love made perfect, that we may have boldness in the day of judgment: because as He is, so are we in this world." I John 4:17

"God is love. When we take up permanent residence in a life of love, we live in God and God lives in us. This way, love has the run of the house, becomes at home and mature in us, so that we're free of worry on Judgment Day-our standing in the world is identical with Christ."
I John 4:17 (The Message Bible)

As indicated by John, love must become mature in us. This means that you must go beyond the confines of just loving those that love you. You must be able to love the Judases of this world.

Can You Love Judas?

Judas, as we know, was one of the original twelve chosen by our Lord. It is also indicated in the scriptures that he was of the devil. Jesus knew this from the start, yet the other disciples did not. What I find so fascinating is the way Jesus treated him during His earthly ministry. Judas was never treated any different than the other disciples. Beloved, this is a powerful picture of how much our love must be demonstrated, even to those considered unworthy of it.

By the example Jesus has left for us, I have concluded in my own heart that mature love does not discriminate. Think about it for a moment. Here was a man that Jesus knew would be the catalyst for betrayal, and ultimately, His demise before the Sanhedrin court. Yet, Jesus never gave any indication that this was Judas' mission until near the end of His earthly ministry. Jesus did not expose him, but rather used Judas' ability to manage the moneybag. Jesus also knew Judas had to fulfill his purpose so He could get where He needed to be, before Pontias Pilate. Why do I bring this point out? Because there are many Judases in our camps. They come with gifts and talents that can benefit the Body of Christ; yet, more often than not, these gifts and talents are not tapped into. If we are to follow the pattern of Jesus Christ, we must learn to deal with Judas. We cannot afford to demonstrate prejudice toward him until the time appointed. None of the disciples ever saw Jesus single him out; on the contrary, they saw the love of Christ toward him, as it was unto them. What a powerful picture of commitment and discipline! Can we love the ones that will certainly betray us? Can we treat them in a way that does not draw attention to their treachery? When we are able to do this, it is evident we are growing up in Christ and are beginning to understand the depth of His love for each of us.

Let me get back to sharing with you my own personal experience with God's love demonstrated. It came at a time when I was carrying a burden for past sin. You see, outwardly I seemed just fine to everyone, but my outward appearance bore a totally different picture than that of my inward disposition. Inwardly I was longing for the Father's love. My selfishness led me away from His hand,

and as a result, I had lived as a spiritual castaway, a fugitive from the land of promise. There is no place more miserable than the one that has you in the realm of make believe. I choose to describe it as make believe, mainly because we go to great lengths to make sure others see us as having everything together, but in secret we know the real deal. We know with certainty if our lives are in alignment with God the Father. His standard is without ambiguity; there are no unrevealed riddles to those who from their hearts seek His will. I was like a little boy needing a great big hug, but no ordinary hug would do. I needed the Father's touch! As I mentioned earlier, I had since long repented, but I still cried out for acceptance among my brothers and sisters. I could not say, all I needed was Jesus, like so many declare today. I needed my brothers and sisters!

My wife and I visited my parents in my hometown (Merrimon). While there, we visited a church called "The City of Refuge" located in Newport, North Carolina. The Senior Pastor, Apostle Willie Murray, is commonly referred to as the Apostle of Love and Unity. God used the Apostle that day to confirm His love and pursuit of me. As the ushers escorted us to the front of the church, I could not help but wonder how I would be received. The Apostle saw us, walked over to me, and without saying a word, embraced and held me in his arms. It was one of the most liberating moments for me; I melted in his arms like a little boy. In that moment, all the weight I was carrying lifted. That small gesture of love and acceptance freed me that day, and I have not forgotten the touch I felt from my heavenly Father through His servant. Life began anew for me because, you see, that day, I knew in my heart that I had been forgiven and accepted. To all of you reading this right now, please, please, never forget, you are an expression of God's love to the wayward that will one day wander down your pathway. Be sure to flow to them from the Most Holy Place. That is, be an instrument through which God reveals His pursuit of them. You will do this by releasing the love of God without judgment or condemnation. To those of you who might be wandering this very moment, God is looking for you. His love has not dissipated with time, neither has it been withdrawn based upon what you have done. His love has remained the same from eternity past. It was in place before the foundation of the world and it will be the same in eternity future. Fall into the arms of a loving Father. He has been after you since you left Him. And make no mistake about it, we all left Him; yet, His love remains. Once you return unto Him, you will understand that His love cannot be compared to any other. Once you feel the warmth of His embrace, it releases you, and encourages you to demonstrate to others what you have experienced. This reminds me of what Isaiah the prophet spoke regarding the love and tenderness of our heavenly Father:

"A bruised reed shall he not break, and the smoking flax shall he not quench." Isaiah 42:3

I challenge you to demonstrate such tenderness toward those wandering and searching. They need to experience what you have, so that they, too, might be free. Glory to God!

There Is Still Hope

We all have met people at one point in our lives that are so far removed from God. We think there is no hope for them. I remind people wherever I go, that as long as that person or persons are still breathing there is hope. No matter how corrupt the lifestyle, there is hope. Jesus left on record that the only sin that would not be forgiven of man is blasphemy of the Holy Ghost. That is, calling the work of the Holy Ghost to be that of the devil. God wants us to acknowledge Him in all our ways; to put Him first in everything, and give Him credit for what He accomplishes through us in this life. We have, also for too long, branded God's work as our own. He has been very clear that He will not share His glory with another. Do you remember Lucifer? He tried claiming God's glory. He tried it and lost, and I mean, he lost huge! God dealt him an eternal blow that he will never recover from. My brothers and sisters, God has no equal, nor is there anyone we can compare Him to, because He is incomparable. He stands alone as the only self-existing God; created by none, yet everyone and everything exists because of Him. Therefore, everything we do must begin and end with Him. When we tend to forget to do this, He will create a tailor made storm for us, not for our destruction, but that we might recall His principle of being first. Start speaking life over those in your circle, those you know to be rebelling against God. No matter how much they have rebelled against God, mercy is still flowing like a river. To receive of this mercy, one only needs to have a change of mind (repentance) and faith toward God.

The Fall and Rise of a King

Consider the Babylonian King, Nebuchadnezzar. In his time there was no earthly king of his equal. He dreamed about a great tree in the earth that was strong, meet for food and shade for all. He also saw a watcher, or angel of God, come down from heaven with a commandment to cut the great tree down; yet, a stump was to be left. He hears these words:

> *"Let his heart be changed from a man's, and let a beast's heart be given unto him; and let seven times (years) pass over him." Daniel 4:16*

The reason for this judgment is to remind the living that God rules in the kingdom of men:

> *"This matter is by the decree of the watchers, and the demand by the word of the holy ones: to the intent that the living may know that the most High ruleth in the kingdom of men, and giveth it to whomsoever he will, and setteth up over it the basest of men." Daniel 4:17*

Think about that for a moment. When we know in our hearts that the Lord our God rules in the kingdom of men, we need not walk in fear, and our dependence certainly will not be in men. There is a peace that comes over us. No matter what the circumstance is, we know in our hearts that it is going to be alright because our God rules in this realm. The words of Apostle Paul are more meaningful to us. He wrote the following to the church in Rome:

"And we know that all things work together for good to them that love God, to them who are the called according to His purpose." Romans 8:28

Daniel reveals to the king that the dream is about him. He informs the king that he will be driven from men and live with beasts of the field. He advises the king to stop sinning by doing righteousness and be merciful to the poor. The Lord gave the king a whole year to change, but he did not. He made a foolish statement about what he accomplished, and God heard him:

"The king spake, and said, is not this great Babylon, that I have built for the house of the kingdom by the might of my power, and for the honour of my majesty? While the word was in the king's mouth, there fell a voice from heaven, saying, O king Nebuchadnezzar, to thee it is spoken; the kingdom is departed from thee." Daniel 4:30-31

From that moment he changed form and lived like a beast in the field, but not without hope. Even when judgment is sure, God's love and grace is even more so. Love and grace is extended to us in the hope that our hearts ripen with repentance and faith toward Him. Daniel recounts the moment of grace upon the king:

> *"Nevertheless leave the stump of his roots in the earth, even with a band of iron and brass, in the tender grass of the field; and let it be wet with the dew of heaven, and let his portion be with the beasts in the grass of the earth." Daniel 4:15*

Wow! Can you see the one who yearns for relationship? God loves us so much, that even when He disciplines us, He provides an avenue back to Him and back to a healthy relationship. How could we ever take credit for the relationship we have with Him? Hear the conclusion of the king, for his experience taught him a valuable lesson it seems we have yet to learn:

> *"Nebuchadnezzar the king unto all the peoples, nations, and languages that dwell in all the earth: Peace be multiplied unto you. It hath seemed good unto me to declare the signs and wonders that the Most High God hath wrought toward me. How great are his signs! and how mighty are his wonders! His kingdom is an everlasting kingdom, and his dominion is from generation to generation." Daniel 4:1-3*

Before you condemn the next person because of how he or she lives, remember your experience with His love and know that there is always hope!

ENDNOTES/SCRIPTURES

1. I John 4:17
2. Isaiah 42:3
3. Romans 8:28
4. Daniel 4:30-31
5. Daniel 4:15-16
6. Daniel 4:1-3

11

GOD'S PROCESS OF HARVEST

*"First the blade, then the ear, after that, the
full corn in the ear."*
Mark 4:28

The Lord left on record how the earth would experience

a harvest; a three-fold harvest, which in my mind speaks

volumes as it relates to our own spiritual harvest. I believe

we, as a people, have missed out on so much that we have

asked God for, mainly because we have misunderstood the

process of His harvest. As a result of misunderstanding the

process, we get frustrated and are persuaded by the spirit of

our adversary that God did not regard our prayer requests.

You see, when the word of God is sown, our adversary is looking to see if we understood it or not. And if we did not, he comes immediately to snatch that word out of our hearts.

"When anyone heareth the word of the kingdom, and understandeth it not, then cometh the wicked one, and catcheth away that which was sown in his heart. This is he which received seed by the way side." Matthew 13:19

Understand my beloved, our adversary's tactics are made plain to us as it pertains to where we are in the Word. He does not waste time getting to those of us with a lack of understanding; however, his assault is somewhat different for those who have exercised themselves in the word at some point. For instance, for those who hear the word and rejoice over it, our adversary has chosen the instruments of tribulation and persecution to make the word ineffective. Then there are others who appear to be extremely grounded, but their focus is too much on the cares of this world and all its riches, thereby, choking the word out, making them unfruitful. So I challenge you to get this word in your spirit, understand it, be changed by it, and bring forth in your realm of ministry. Now, let's get back to the process of harvest:

> *"For the earth bringeth forth fruit of herself; first the blade, then the ear, after that the full corn in the ear." Mark 4:28*

Jesus said the kingdom of God was similar to a man sowing seed, and though he rises and falls every day, he knoweth not how the seed grows. God does not need our help to produce; He needs our obedience to bring it forth for us, for our benefit, and for the benefit of the world. He states that the first sign out of the ground is not a harvest, but rather the blade. Let's explore this for a moment and see how it is relevant to believers today.

First the Blade

As I mentioned, the process of harvest is three-fold; first, the blade. Consider a man having no transportation. During his prayer time he asked God to bless him with a Cadillac. Shortly thereafter, a co-worker who owned numerous vehicles had a Chevrolet Chevette that he was not using, so he blessed the individual with it. The Chevette is a far cry from the Cadillac. However, in the process of

God's harvest, it is the blade. This individual, because of a lack of understanding, believes that God has not heard his cry. On the contrary, the God of Heaven did hear his cry; the blade is evident of it. Beloved, the blade was the evidence that God heard and answered his prayer. He is

sending a message that the harvest is on its way. Due to the lack of understanding, the man mistreated the Chevette (blade), never washed it or performed routine maintenance on it. The Chevette eventually broke down and the man was without transportation again. What happened? He proved that not only did he not understand God's process, but that he was not ready for the harvest he asked for. God wanted to see how he would treat the blade. If he understood God's process of harvest, he would have taken care of the Chevette as though it was the Cadillac.

Then the Ear

Let's say the individual understood the process and

treated the Chevette as if it was the Cadillac. If this was the case, along the way, the ear would have shown up. Maybe a friend was getting rid of a Toyota Camry and thought of the man and presented it to him as a gift, or sold it to him at such a discounted price that it was just like giving it away. The Toyota Camry (ear) is a move closer to full harvest. He treats the Camry as if it was indeed the Cadillac. People marvel at how well he maintains it. This is key to every level in our maturity in Christ.

Full Corn in the Ear

After a while, the man is led to visit a Cadillac dealership, where he sees the car of his dreams. In his mind he thinks that it is out of his reach, but on this day they have a special going on and he qualifies for the special package. After a few hours at the dealership, the man is driving away with the Cadillac (Full Corn), he asked God for.

Many of you may be frustrated because you have asked God for something that has yet to materialize. I ask you to take a moment of pause and think about it. Look around you. Have some things just showed up in your life that is perhaps on a smaller scale, but certainly, in the ball park of what you asked for? How well have you kept and maintained it? You may have asked God for a four bedroom house, but not yet realized the importance of taking care of the two bedroom apartment. Before you give place to the devil, settle down long enough to see if you have indeed received from the Lord. It's amazing we can have the evidence in our hands that full harvest is on its way, but because of a lack of understanding, we mistreat what we have, not knowing the signal it is sending to our God. Harvest is coming; in fact, you may already have the evidence.

In everything God does, He does for our good. I am glad the Lord has, by in large, set forth a three-fold process to harvest. Using as an illustration how the earth brings forth is genius. The earth's process will always remain constant, that is, you will not plant a tomato plant today and go out the next day and see ripe tomatoes on it. It will take time; it must endure the course God has set for its production. Likewise, I believe if we received everything all at once, it would certainly be our undoing. We must endure God's process of harvest.

An Old Testament principle of harvest is found in the Book of Exodus:

"I will send my fear before thee, and will destroy all the people to whom thou shalt come, and I will make all thine enemies turn their backs unto thee. And I will send hornets before thee, which shall drive out the Hivite, the Canaanite, and the Hittite, from before thee. I will not drive them out from before thee in one year; lest the land become desolate, and the beast of the field multiply against thee. By little and little I will drive them out from before thee, until thou be increased, and inherit the land." Exodus 23:27-30

God promised to gradually give the land to the people of Israel. The purpose for this was simple, Israel would not have been prepared to settle in and maintain it. The Lord said if He had given it to them to quickly, the land would become desolate, and run over with the beast of the field. God reveals His wisdom and love by not driving the enemy out too quickly. His people were not ready; they had not grown into a people that could handle the whole land.

The same can be said about us today. We would not take a 45-caliber pistol, give it to a three year old, and expect the child not to pull the trigger. Curiosity would overtake the child and he or she would eventually pull the trigger. As loving parents, we would not give a child access to something they are not responsible enough to manage or control.

I believe Apostle Paul best sums up the principle of harvest in his address to the Church in Galatia:

> *"Now I say, that the heir, as long as he is a child, differeth nothing from a servant, though he be lord of all. But is under tutors and governors until the time appointed of the father." Galatians 4:1-2*

We have a loving Father who also wants to make sure we can handle that which He desires to put in our hands.

ENDNOTES/SCRIPTURES

1. Matthew 13:19
2. Mark 4:28
3. Exodus 23:27-30
4. Galatians 4:1-2

12

THE WORTH OF A SOUL

"Go ye therefore, teach all nations."
Matthew 28:19

Throughout this book I endeavored to focus your attention on the fact that God initiates, and He is the one capable of maintaining, a true relationship with His people. Seeing the steps the Lord has taken to redeem us, let us be like-minded when it comes to the lengths we will go to win souls for His kingdom. Prior to His departure from the earth, He left on record these final words:

> *"All power is given unto me in heaven and in earth.*
> *Go ye therefore, and teach all nations."*
> *Matthew 28:18-19*

Seeing that all authority finds its resting place in Him, we are to be focused on His heart's desire, and that is winning souls. He has given to us the ministry and the word necessary to reconcile the world.

> *"And all things are of God, who hath reconciled us to himself by Jesus Christ, and hath given to us the ministry of reconciliation. To wit, that God was in Christ, reconciling the world unto himself, not imputing their trespasses unto them; and hath committed unto us the word of reconciliation."*
> *II Corinthians 5:18-19*

> *"All this comes from the God who settled the relationship between us and him, and then called us to settle our relationships with each other. God put the world square with himself through the Messiah, giving the world a fresh start by offering forgiveness of sins. God has given us the task of telling everyone what he is doing."*
> *II Corinthians 5:18-19 (The Message Bible)*

I want to focus your attention on one word the apostle used to describe the work of the Lord, and this is the word "reconciliation." This word means to cause to be friendly and harmonious again. The Lord is sending the message to us that we were at one point in a friendly and harmonious relationship with Him. We were in God before time; we entered this world under the bondage and corruption of sin.

Through Christ Jesus, He has brought us back to God. I like how The Message Bible puts it; God put the world square with Himself. As a result of being square with Him, He has given us the ministry to reach out to those that have yet to come to know what He has done. Go tell someone today that through the work of Jesus, they are square with God. All they have to do is repent and accept His atonement.

The Lord Jesus Christ commanded that we should go and make disciples. There are many out there in the world waiting to be made into another person. Beloved, many are wandering and they have no idea that God is after them. Choose to be His reflection of love and compassion to them today. In light of this challenge, I want to share with you a word that was passed along to me in the 1980s. God used W.K. Norton, a missionary to India, to leave this message on record. It was recorded in 1923, but its relevance remains to this day. I have printed it in its entirety in the hope that it will stir your heart for what God wants, and that is the lost souls of this world. The title of his writing is

"The Worth of A Soul."

The worth of a soul! Who can count its value? Who can appraise its worth? An immortal soul is beyond all price. In money, one soul is of more value than the wealth of the whole world. In suffering, it is better that all the people of the world would suffer all their lives on earth, if by their suffering one soul could be saved. In journeying, no foreign land is too distant or any portion of it too in accessible, for all the people of the world to take a journey there, if by so doing one soul could be saved.

There is no trouble too great, no humiliation too deep, no suffering too severe, no love too strong, no labor too hard, no expense too large, but that is worth it, if it is spent in the effort to win a soul. Of all the creations in this world and in the world to come, the greatest, the most wonderful, the most priceless, the most enduring is a soul.

God loves the soul more than all other creation. He fashioned it after His own image, and made it like unto

Himself. Every soul has departed from God and gone astray, and God has brought every soul back again with a price. That price was the blood of His only begotten Son, who took upon Himself the sin of the soul, suffered the death penalty, that the soul might be saved, cleansed, and made holy again. God loves every soul with an everlasting, eternal love greater and deeper than any human love can possibly be.

Satan hates the soul. In satan's enmity towards God, he is using all his energy, using every snare, his utmost cunning, employing every means with one single purpose of ruining the soul of man, because satan knows the soul is God's most cherished creation, the very apple of His eye. A soul will never die.

When the earth of ours has crumbled to dust, and has passed away into the forgotten past, a soul will still be in its freshness of youth. When in the fathomless future eternity has become hoary with age, the soul will still be young. When million, million eternities have each lived out their endless ages and have rolled by into the unthinkable past, and time is no more, the soul will still be living, a conscious personal reality, endowed with perpetual youth and perpetual life. God has said: "He that winneth souls is wise."

If Christians would only realize the value and the immortality of a soul, and the shortness of this earthly life, they would work feverishly, unceasingly, with all their greatest energy, day after day, year after year that they might save one. O Christians, are there souls passing your way? Are you bestirring yourself in their behalf that they may have eternal life and joy, or are you allowing them to cross your path and pass unwarned, to an eternal death?

W.K. Norton, Missionary to India (1923)

ENDNOTES/SCRIPTURES

1. Matthew 28.19
2. II Corinthians 5:18-19
3. Worth of A Soul by W.K. Norton

Dr. Lewis Fisher, Jr.
www.LewisFisherJr.com

Is Available To Speak At Your Event!
For More Information, Contact Dr. Lewis Fisher, Jr.

757-374-3872
Author@GodsPursuitOfYou.com

Please Share Your Testimony Of How
God's Pursuit Of You
Impacted And Empowered Your Life!

SpeakLife Publishing

Do you need a publisher for your well-written Christian faith-based non-fiction book, but don't know where to start?

Contact SpeakLife Publishing Today!
1-888-596-3882
We coach you from concept to completion!

"That I may publish with the voice of thanksgiving and tell of all Thy wondrous works!"
Psalms 26:7

Proof

Made in the USA
Charleston, SC
28 April 2012